Marsha G. Witten is Assistant Professor of Sociology at Franklin and Marshall College.

D0205398

All Is Forgiven

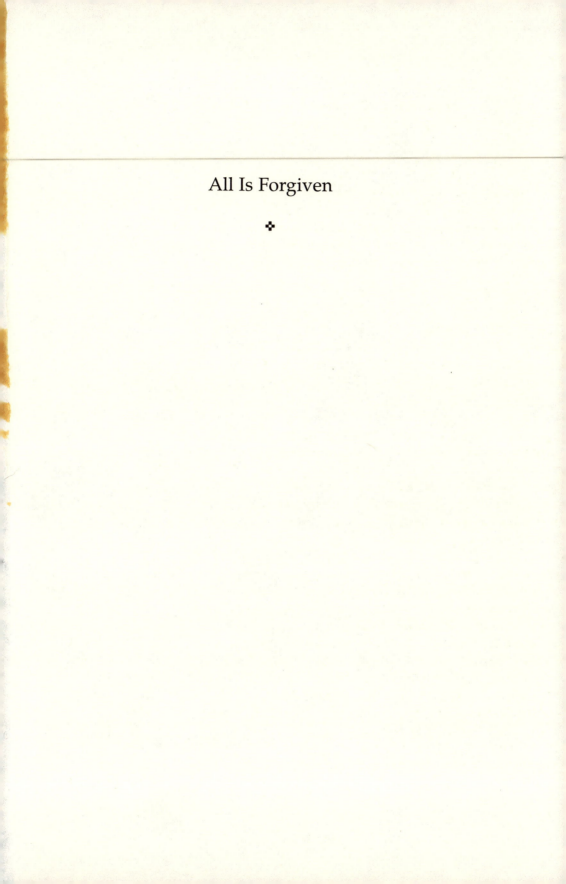

All Is Forgiven

THE SECULAR MESSAGE
IN AMERICAN PROTESTANTISM

✤

Marsha G. Witten

PRINCETON UNIVERSITY PRESS

PRINCETON, NEW JERSEY

Library of Congress Cataloging-in-Publication Data
Witten, Marsha Grace.
All is forgiven : the secular message
in American Protestantism / Marsha G. Witten.
p. cm.
Includes bibliographical references and index.
ISBN 0-691-03280-7
1. Protestant churches—United States—Doctrines—History—20th century.
2. Secularization (Theology)—History of doctrines—19th century.
3. Preaching—United States—History—20th century.   4. Prodigal son (Parable).
5. Sermons, American—History and criticism.   6. United States—Church history—
20th century.   I. Title.
BR526.W58   1993
251′00973—dc20   93-4048   CIP

Grateful acknowledgment is given to the following for permission
to reprint selections from their sermons:
Murrill N. Boitnott, Les Borsay, Jack C. Burton, Dr. Ron Lee Davis, Lewis M. Evans,
D.D., Dr. S. Allen Foster, Brian Harbour, Bernard R. Hawley, Wallace David Moore,
W. Dan Parker, James Madison Ramsey, David S. Reiter, W. James Richards,
Michael D. Riley, H. Stephen Shoemaker, Dr. Robert B. Smith,
William G. Southerland, Laird Stuart,
and twenty-nine pastors who wish to remain anonymous.

TO MY FAMILY

❖

❖ *Contents* ❖

❖ *Acknowledgments* ❖

THIS BOOK has resulted from the generosity of many people. I owe thanks to the pastors of the Presbyterian Church (U.S.A.) and the Southern Baptist Convention who responded to my request by sending me a sermon on Luke 15. Princeton University funded the doctoral studies that led to this book and awarded me the Harold W. Dodds Fellowship in my final year. Nancy Ammerman, Marvin Bressler, Kevin Christiano, Thomas Long, Albert Raboteau, Christine Smith, and John Wilson were extremely helpful at the beginning stages of this project.

The following people gave me valuable insights into the sermons: Philip Bakelaar, Michael Billig, David Brown, Cindy Gibson, Susan Harding, Carol Harris-Shapiro, Christopher Lynch, Mark Pollock, Anita Pomerantz, and David Watt. Thanks go also to participants in the Workshop in Religion and American Culture at Princeton University, in the session on social scientific analyses of religion at the mid-Atlantic meeting of the American Academy of Religion (1992), and in the Colloquium of the Department of Rhetoric and Communication at Temple University. In addition, Martin Bradley, Richard Gladden, Norman Green, Brian Horton, Glenn Koch, Jack Marcum, John Schmidt, Laura Schwartz, Pat Strum, and Barbie Zelizer provided advice and information that have made this a stronger work.

I am grateful to the following people for commenting on part or all of the manuscript at various stages: Jeffrey Alexander, Marvin Bressler, Gene Burns, George Cheney, N.J. Demerath III, Robert Handy, Susan Harding, Tricia Jones, Thomas Long, James Moorhead, Alan Neely, Mark Noll, and Herbert Simons. Ann Himmelberger Wald, Religion Editor at Princeton University Press, not only guided this project to fruition but also gave very useful comments during revision of the manuscript. All errors, it goes without saying, are mine alone.

A few people should be singled out for thanks: Robert Wuthnow, for guidance and inspiration; Michèle Lamont, for counsel and support; Eva Garroutte, for insight and friendship; Herbert Bass, for editorial expertise; my parents, Bernice and Carl Witten, for assistance and love; my husband, Charles Slater, for advice and encouragement, and for putting up with it all; and our son, Benjamin, for teaching me, through his presence in our lives, something about miracles.

All Is Forgiven

❖

CHAPTER ONE

Protestant Preaching
in Contemporary American Culture

O<small>N THE AFTERNOON</small> of Good Friday, 1990, I sat in my living room listening to a broadcast of J. S. Bach's *St. Matthew Passion* performed by the Consort of Early Instruments. The stark sonorities of the original instruments used in the performance, and the weak, still unfulfilled sunshine of eastern Pennsylvania's early spring, seemed to heighten the pathos of the events portrayed in Bach's setting of the gospel text: an account, plain and unelaborated, and unaccompanied by elements of hope or joy, of the sufferings and crucifixion of Jesus. Just as the sublime final chorale began, with antiphonal choirs calling out sorrowfully to Jesus in his grave, I heard the familiar thump outside the door that signaled the arrival of the day's mail. As the performance ended, I went to the mailbox and opened the thickest envelope in it. The letter it contained was from a local Baptist church in the process of formation. This is the message that greeted me from that church on that Good Friday:

> Hi Neighbor!
>
> At last! A new church for those who have given up on church services! Let's face it. Many people aren't active in church these days.
> WHY?
> Too often
> · the sermons are boring and don't relate to daily living
> · many churches seem more interested in your wallet than in you
> · members are unfriendly to visitors
> · you wonder about the quality of the nursery care for your little ones
> Do you think attending church should be enjoyable?
> WELL, WE'VE GOT GOOD NEWS FOR YOU!
> Valley Church is a new church designed to meet your needs in the 1990's. At Valley Church you
> · meet new friends and get to know your neighbors

· enjoy exciting music with a contemporary flavor
· hear positive, practical messages which uplift you each week
    How to feel good about yourself
    How to overcome depression
    How to have a full and successful life
    Learning to handle your money without it handling you
    The secrets of successful family living
    How to overcome stress
· trust your children to the care of dedicated nursery workers
  WHY NOT GET A LIFT INSTEAD OF A LETDOWN THIS
SUNDAY?[1]

The Paradox of Protestantism

This conjunction of event and text is probably as jarring to read about now as it was for me to experience at the time. On the one hand, a radio station in a major U.S. city dramatizes the meaning of Good Friday by airing Bach's intensely spiritual rendition of the suffering and fallen Jesus, drawn in the stark words of Matthew's Gospel. On the other hand, a burgeoning church congregation in a suburb of that city times its mass mailing of a form letter and brochure to reach potential adherents on the same Christian holy day. Mimicking the slick direct-mail solicitation of a credit card or insurance company, the letter contains a cheerful, practical list of the social and psychological pleasures one might receive from affiliation within its church—with no mention whatsoever of faith or God, let alone of suffering or spiritual striving.

These two discourses seem to form an opposition: the spirituality, the struggle of faith, and the sublime image of God in the first message; and the optimistic, untroubled, purely mundane, communication of the second. The messages seem contradictory, providing incompatible versions of what religion can (or should) entail. Yet both are public pronouncements about Christianity, about faith, and about the place of religion in contemporary American life. Taken together, they tell us much about the state of Christianity, and specifically, its Protestant forms, within American culture in the late twentieth century.

As we shall see, the seeming incongruity of these messages—the juxtaposition of the spiritual and the psychological, the transcendent and the pragmatic—paints an accurate portrait of contemporary Protestant

4

faith and practice. This portrait is the Janus face of apparent paradox: one side bearing the visage of traditional piety, the other the face of secularity. The front side of the picture reminds us that there are many indications of a maintained, even resurgent, religious orientation among American Protestants (as among U.S. Catholics and Jews).[2] But the nether side testifies to indications that modern Protestantism in the United States has been greatly influenced by general trends toward secularity, specifically by tendencies toward individualism, trust in psychotherapy, ideological relativism, and reliance on rational procedures that mark our culture as a whole.

This book examines the paradox of Protestantism in late-twentieth-century American culture through a case study of contemporary sermons of pastors of two major U.S. denominations, the Presbyterian Church (U.S.A.) and the Southern Baptist Convention. I focus on the religious and social themes that figure most prominently in the sermons: images of God; conceptions of the Christian's place in the world; notions of sin and the sinful person; and doctrines of human nature and the transformation of the self through conversion. As I analyze the language of the sermons, I discuss the ways in which the texts display the tensions that contemporary American culture provides for religious pronouncements. In addition, I demonstrate how religious speakers use the various styles of speech available to them—spiritual and secular, traditional and contemporary—in attempts to resolve the dilemmas of religion in modern American life.

Religion and Secularity

Not long ago, sociologists tended to look at Western religion through the lens of the "secularization thesis." The term was used to label and explain the processes whereby, supposedly, religion is increasingly eviscerated by secular forces in the modern world.[3] Briefly put, the secularization thesis goes as follows: Within the context of increasing modernization, religion undergoes two crucial changes. First, its authority is narrowed to an ever-diminishing realm, as social institutions differentiate from religion and rely upon alternative legitimations.[4] Second, the small social space left for sacred things becomes marked by the very instrumental reason that defines the conduct of public life in the secular sphere.[5] Thus constrained and compromised, religion

5

is rendered less and less plausible in the public sphere, and its influence decreases in the private sphere as well.[6] The most pessimistic proponents of a theory of linear secularization—notably, Max Weber—predicted the ever-diminishing influence of religion in modern affairs.[7]

Religious Responses to Modernity

Contemporary scholars who examine the effects of secularity on religion no longer posit the straightforward decline that Weber anticipated. Instead, theorists believe that American religion will survive as an important social institution, as data about church attendance and religious belief suggest. But, they think, secularity is affecting the internal contents of religion—its ideology, speech, and practice—forcing it to undergo serious changes.[8] In this view, modern culture exacts a toll from traditional religious beliefs, articulations, and behavior, elbowing religious tenets and pronouncements into increasing conformity with the norms of the secular world. Topics of elemental religious concern— the nature of God and his relationship to humankind, the problem of sin and the hope of salvation, the configuration of the individual person and responsibility to the community, explanation for evil and comfort for suffering—all are subject to adaptation as religion strives to make its place within modern secular culture.

But "accommodation" to secularity, as I term speech strategies of adaptation, is not the only response that religious speakers can make to the challenges of contemporary culture. As some scholars suggest, moves toward the accommodation of religion to secular culture provoke countermoves from other religious practitioners. Using a set of strategies I term "resistance," these practitioners may rebuff secular forces, denying, debunking, or neutralizing the influences of modernity in their speech. Or they may chart new paths between the two extreme responses by redefining religion in ways that show a contemporary self-awareness about the power of language use, strategies I term "reframing." These strategies include separating symbols from meaning and reflecting critically on one's own pronouncements.[9]

These speculations suggest a promising avenue for examining contemporary religion. They engage our interest in Protestant speech as part of an ongoing process: the struggle to resolve the tensions among the various strands of influence within modern American culture and within the historical experience of the denominations. This is a struggle in which many of today's Protestant churches are involved.

FACING THE CHALLENGES OF SECULARITY

The two denominations whose sermons are studied here—the Presbyterian Church (U.S.A.) and the Southern Baptist Convention—are among those that are markedly aware of the implications of modern life for their beliefs and practices. The debates that are raging in both denominations directly touch on these issues. What is an authentic discourse for Protestant religion in American culture of the late twentieth century? How can the churches draw on their resources of speech to cut a trail through the thickets of secularity? As they labor to find answers to these questions, the two denominations cast in sharp relief the problems of much of contemporary mainline Protestantism.

At first glance, we might conclude that the Presbyterian Church (U.S.A) and the Southern Baptist Convention have been affected quite differently by their encounter with secularity. A Reformed tradition, rooted in a strict interpretation of Calvinism, American Presbyterianism has experienced many conflicts between conservative and liberal theological contingents over the years. (A brief discussion of the history of the two denominations is given in Appendix One.) The denominational affiliation of approximately 2.6 million Americans in 1990,[10] the Presbyterian Church (U.S.A.) appears to be a textbook case of the decline that has struck hard at mainstream Protestantism. It has lost approximately 30 percent of its membership since 1966.[11] The "graying" of the remaining membership has forced a slowdown in some congregations to the generation of creative new programs.[12]

The denomination appears to be in the throes of a massive identity crisis. Many of the marks of its traditional denominational self-definition that have differentiated Presbyterianism from other Protestant groups in the United States have been lost in recent years. The demographics of Presbyterian membership have become virtually indistinguishable from those of other Protestant churches, and the commitment of the denomination to ecumenism has eroded unique features of Presbyterian doctrine and practice.[13] Further, there is much internal dissension about theological and practical priorities. Concluding that the emphasis on social action in the decades since the 1960s may have gone too far, some church leaders are wondering whether the denomination should resume its traditional evangelistic mission and place less stress on social concerns. And, given the mixed heritage of the denomination, acrimonious debates are frequently joined over such theologically loaded "lifestyle" issues as abortion and sexual practices. For example, in the summer of 1991, the governing body of the Presbyterian Church (U.S.A.) overwhelmingly defeated adoption of a report that would ease sanctions against sexual relationships among gays and lesbians and unmarried heterosexuals, against the protests of a vocal opposition.[14]

On the other hand, the Southern Baptist Convention has been led for more than a decade by a powerful fundamentalist wing. It is heir to a strong tradition of conservative theology, with a long-standing emphasis on evangelism. Although membership growth is small, the denomination is not suffering the attrition that plagues other mainline groups, and is currently the denominational choice of more than 15 million Americans.[15] The expansion of the denomination into regions outside the South, which began in the late 1940s, continues, as new congregations are founded even in the seemingly alien turf of New England.

Yet Southern Baptists are struggling to define themselves, too, as theological and social factions within the denomination contest for authority. Although fundamentalists seem firmly in control of the Convention's apparatus, and although their stance on biblical inerrancy was officially adopted in 1987, the debates over biblical interpretation that have been joined for the last two decades between conservatives and moderates have spawned dissident factions.[16] Recently, those who object to the fundamentalists' theological and structural control over the Convention have formalized their opposition by establishing a fellowship of their own, intending to work toward their own set of goals.[17] The fellowship allows churches to bypass the fundamentalist-controlled central organization in contributing to funding of Southern Baptist mission programs.[18] Such attempts to countervail fundamentalist forces are likely to multiply in the future, as the expansion of Southern Baptist churches proceeds outward from the South into other regions of the country, from rural areas into cities and suburbs, and from the lower classes into groups of middle-class and professional people. Although the rifts are relatively recent, they mark a dilemma for the Southern Baptist Convention as it confronts the forces of modernity.

Thus, despite the seeming differences between the two denominations, it is certain that for both, the most pressing problem of the last decade of the twentieth century is to work out positions defining attitudes and practices in response to the secular world. As these denominations reach for ideological resources to work through their internal and external disputes, as they address issues of theological and practical concern, members of the denominations have available to them both contemporary and historical resources of speech.

Sociological Studies of Culture
through Language

The recent heightening of attention to cultural issues within sociology has spurred an interest in the cultural function of language. Scholars have turned their attention to the role of language in such varied social processes as power and authority in the workplace, the establishment of "knowledge" in the practices of science, the dilemmas of public policy choice that attend such ethical issues as abortion, and the core values and goals of the American people.[19] In so doing, they have added to our understanding of the social uses of discourse: constructing and communicating ideas and beliefs, symbolizing self and communities, and modeling ideologies and behaviors.

Some contemporary sociological examinations of mainline American Protestantism implicitly acknowledge the centrality of language to religious communities. Rarely, however, do they treat the speech of religious participants as a major topic. Recent participant-observation studies, such as those by Nancy Ammerman, Randall Balmer, Alan Peshkin, Steven Tipton, and Steven Warner, include insightful discussions of the speech of the practitioners they investigate, but do not focus systematically on language use.[20] James Hunter provides a discerning analysis of some recent popular evangelical texts, but does not fully plumb the richness of the discourse.[21] Researchers who use techniques of survey sampling have examined isolated religious themes that emerge from the responses of religious practitioners, but their need to reduce the themes to simple categories for the purposes of statistical analysis masks the complexity of the speech involved.[22] In fact, social scientific interest in contemporary religious speech appears to be limited largely to groups outside the mainstream of American life—for

9

example, new religious movements, the Protestantism of rural African-Americans, and the charismatic practices of people who live in Appalachia.[23] Yet even these studies are limited in focus, since they deal with single religious issues such as the language of the conversion appeal or the reconstruction of identity in the talk of cults or marginal movements, or as they concentrate on identifying speech styles without reference to the larger culture.[24]

Because speech has been neglected as a topic in the sociology of religion, analytical techniques for studying religious talk are generally unrefined. There are, however, models from work in other areas of sociology and in related disciplines to which a researcher concerned with issues of religious language can turn. Ann Swidler provides an apt metaphor for conceiving of language use in her reconceptualization of culture as a "tool kit" of resources from which members draw to construct meanings in different social circumstances. The social analysts of *Habits of the Heart* demonstrate how attention to specific vocabularies of American speech sheds light on the construction of core values and beliefs in modern society. Similarly, Donal Carbaugh examines American registers of speech about the self through the lens of popular culture. Looking at Baptist conversion from the perspective of rhetorical performance, Susan Harding investigates how conversion works in the context of contemporary culture. And Robert Wuthnow notes the need to see religious discourse as an important example of public rhetoric that calls for thorough, systematic analysis.[25]

SERMONS IN AMERICAN PROTESTANTISM

The context for my examination of religious speech is the venerable Protestant genre of the sermon. Preaching traditionally has held pride of place in the main currents of American Protestantism. Throughout American history, the diminished emphasis on liturgy that characterizes both Lutheran and Reformed traditions has tended to highlight the religious function of the sermon. Articulating doctrine, interpreting Scripture, exhorting sinners to convert, admonishing those already saved to change their behavior, rendering comfort and advice, the sermon has traditionally been seen as the central vehicle in mainline faith communities for proclaiming the Christian message.[26] In Puritan New England, where the sermon was also the only regular, reliable source of public information, it was not unusual for preachers to deliver addresses lasting two hours or more. In fact, one scholar has calculated that, over the course of a lifetime, the average Puritan listened to nearly fifteen thousand hours of sermonizing.[27] As the great waves of Protestant revivalism flooded American society in subsequent centuries, evangelical pastors and lay preachers suffused first New England and then frontier areas with impassioned appeals for conversion.[28] Any account of major religious figures in the United States should include such Protestant preachers as John Cotton, Jonathan Edwards, Charles Finney, Richard Allen, Henry Beecher, Phebe Palmer, Russell Conwell, Dwight Moody, Walter Rauschenbusch, Aimee Semple McPherson, Harry Emerson Fosdick, Charles Tindley, Norman Vincent Peale, Billy Graham, and Martin Luther King, Jr. Today, as the demographics of both pulpit and congregations change, as contemporary theologies highlight nontraditional concerns, and as pastors strive to reach audiences effectively, many theologians and practitioners show renewed interest in understanding the dynamics of preaching.[29]

The mainline Protestant sermon remains the centerpiece of the worship service. Although they are frequently laden with a host of other duties, contemporary pastors take preaching seriously. They are likely to give substantial thought and time to preparing their sermons, whether they write them out word for word, preach from outlines, or just make a few notes as an aid to speaking. In mainline churches, the language of preaching is, in general, careful and deliberative even when mixed with emotion and enthusiasm. In addition, although preaching usually takes the form of a monologue, rather than a conversation or argument with parishioners, the speaker usually is sensitive to the pulse of the congregation. While pastors may prod congregants in certain directions, most know what is acceptable to their listeners.

For these reasons, and because the length of the sermon (on average, twenty to thirty minutes) and normative structure (elaboration of two or more points using a variety of speech genres) allow the researcher ample talk upon which to work, the analysis of sermons is ideal for the purposes of this study.

The Parable of the Prodigal Son

The sermons examined in this book center around the same scriptural passage: a parable, or teaching story, of Jesus that appears in the New Testament Gospel of Luke (chapter 15, verses 11–32). The text is commonly referred to as the Parable of the Prodigal, or Lost, Son. It occurs as the last episode in a series of three short parables about lost things: The first is about a lost sheep, and the second, about a lost coin, whose owners go to great lengths to find them. According to Luke, Jesus is surrounded by tax collectors and sinners as he speaks; his words are overheard by Pharisees and scribes.

The parable reads as follows:

> And [Jesus] said, "There was a man who had two sons; and the younger of them said to his father, 'Father, give me the share of property that falls to me.' And he divided his living between them.
>
> Not many days later, the younger son gathered all he had and took his journey into a far country, and there he squandered his property in loose living.
>
> And when he had spent everything, a great famine arose in that country, and he began to be in want.
>
> So he went and joined himself to one of the citizens of that country, who sent him into his fields to feed swine.
>
> And he would gladly have fed on the pods that the swine ate; and no one gave him anything.
>
> But when he came to himself he said, 'How many of my father's hired servants have bread enough and to spare, but I perish here with hunger!
>
> I will arise and go to my father, and I will say to him, "Father, I have sinned against heaven and before you;
>
> I am no longer worthy to be called your son; treat me as one of your hired servants." '
>
> And he arose and came to his father. But while he was yet at a distance, his father saw him and had compassion, and ran and embraced him and kissed him.
>
> And the son said to him, 'Father, I have sinned against heaven and before you. I am no longer worthy to be called your son.'
>
> But the father said to his servants, 'Bring quickly the best robe, and put it on him; and put a ring on his hand, and shoes on his feet; and bring the fatted calf and kill it, and let us eat and make merry; for this my son was dead, and is alive again; he was lost, and is found.' And they began to make merry.
>
> Now his elder son was in the field; and as he came and drew near to the house, he heard music and dancing.
>
> And he called one of the servants and asked what this meant.

And he said to him, 'Your brother has come, and your father has killed
the fatted calf, because he has received him safe and sound.'

But he was angry and refused to go in. His father came out and en-
treated him, but he answered his father, 'Lo, these many years I
have served you, and I never disobeyed your command; yet you
never gave me a kid, that I might make merry with my friends.

But when this son of yours came, who has devoured your living with
harlots, you killed for him the fatted calf.'

And he said to him, 'Son, you are always with me, and all that is mine
is yours.

It was fitting to make merry and be glad, for this your brother was
dead, and is alive; he was lost, and is found.'"

(Revised Standard Version)

How the Study Was Conducted

The study presented in this book is based on the texts of forty-seven
sermons on Luke 15:11–32 preached between 1986 and 1988 by a sample of pastors within the Presbyterian Church (U.S.A.) and the Southern Baptist Convention. I obtained the sermons by writing to 150 pastors of large churches within each denomination, asking them to send
a recent message on the Parable of the Prodigal Son. Of the forty-seven
sermons that could be used in the analysis, twenty-one are from Southern Baptists and twenty-six from Presbyterians. Here, I briefly discuss
the conduct of the study; the details appear in Appendix Two.

I decided to solicit sermons on this parable for several reasons. First,
since it has a long history as a central text of Protestant preaching and
commentary, the pastors in my sample were likely to have preached on
it.[30] In addition, I wanted a text that the speakers would favor and
enjoy treating in their sermons. Many of the covering letters that accompanied the manuscripts they sent me indicated that this hunch was
correct—in fact, pastors tend to place special importance on preaching
this parable, and for many, it is a favorite text. Also, I wanted a text
with no obvious interpretation: a text that does not contain within itself
an explicit resolution of meaning. The purpose, of course, was to find
a text that invites a variety of treatments and interpretations. Again I
was not disappointed. The sermons interpret the parable in numerous
ways. Some focus exclusively on explicating the text, while others only

touch on it tangentially on their way to other themes; some emphasize the family drama, while others dwell on the individual characters. For some preachers, the message derives its meaning from contextualization within Luke as a whole, and particularly from the series of three parables that constitute Luke 15; for others, the story is self-contained and needs no scriptural context. Some favor the point of view of the prodigal son, others of the older brother, and still others of the father.

The study was designed to sample only large churches for both substantive and practical reasons. It is from the better established and more influential preachers that the central patterns of speech may be discovered, and these preachers are more likely to be found in the larger churches.[31] In addition, large churches are more likely to have the resources for maintaining files of past sermons.

The design does impose certain limitations on the study, but I do not think any is critical. First, the analysis focuses only on the texts of the sermons, and ignores issues of delivery—what rhetorical scholars would call their paraverbal and nonverbal features (for example, intonation, rate of speaking, and gestures and other movements). Because I did not study the sermons' actual performances as preaching events, it is likely that I missed aspects of their rhetorical force. A complete analysis of preaching style would need to take these characteristics into account. But since the aims of this research are limited to an examination of the sermons' contents, the analysis was not harmed by neglecting aspects of delivery.[32]

In addition, the focus on large churches omits women from the Presbyterian sample. This is the price to pay, unfortunately, for examining central tendencies in sermon speech, since women have not yet had time markedly to penetrate the pastoral leadership of the denomination. (The Southern Baptist sample includes no women, either, as the great majority of the Convention's churches do not ordain them.)[33]

Another caveat concerns a possible bias in the sampling of Southern Baptist pastors. A focus on large churches may have tapped a greater proportion of theologically moderate (as opposed to conservative or fundamentalist) preachers than is representative of the denomination as a whole.[34] While this is a valid concern, it is somewhat mitigated by the goal of the study: to look for general patterns of speech, not to make arguments based on statistical analysis.[35]

There is also the limitation imposed on this study by the choice of a single sermon from each pastor, based on the same biblical text, as the data for analysis. Because on a commonsensical reading the Parable of the Prodigal Son appears to emphasize forgiveness for wrongdoing, it might be argued that we are seeing interpretations of some aspects of the parable—particularly the nature of God and sin—that are more artifacts of the choice of biblical text than representations of the general tendencies of Presbyterian and Southern Baptist preaching.

We should be careful, therefore, not to overread these findings. At the same time, it is extremely important to note that the images of God and sin that appear in these sermons are consonant with pronounced tendencies in contemporary Protestant thought in general that have been observed by researchers. For example, Andrew Greeley reports that nearly three quarters of respondents in a survey in the mid-1980s preferred the image of God as "friend" to that of him as "king."[36] Surveys by the Gallup Organization show that most Americans think of God as loving them, and only a small minority say they have ever been afraid of him.[37] And James Hunter has documented the tendency of the popular evangelical literature he studied to stress God's therapeutic role, to downplay notions of sin, and to highlight the accessibility of forgiveness and conversion.[38] Thus, it seems likely that the effect of the preaching text is more to underscore particular tendencies of interpretation that are generally present than to create interpretations idiosyncratic to this parable.

Finally, this study is circumscribed by examining sermons from only two denominations, and only forty-seven sermons in all. Surely a larger sample would have permitted broader conclusions to be drawn. But a limited study was made necessary by my choice of methods of analysis, which allowed me to examine in detail every part of every sermon. This would not have been feasible with a substantially larger sample. Given the scarcity of studies focusing on religious language, I decided it was more important to examine the language of the sermons in depth than to cast a broader net, which would have forced me to analyze speech more superficially.[39]

I used methods of structured discourse analysis to examine the sermons. Discourse analytic studies look for patterns in talk and text and aim to describe properties of language in use.[40] These methods allow the texts to speak for themselves to the greatest extent possible, instead of imposing a preexisting analytical scheme on them. In addition, they force the analyst to pay attention not only to major themes but also to nuances of expression. In practice, this means that I allowed the topics of substantive concern and the categories under each topic to emerge from the texts themselves, and that I analyzed all parts of all of the sermons in my sample.

I have considered the sermons not from the viewpoint of a theologian or religious practitioner but from that of a sociologist. How has this affected my understanding of the religious subject matter of the texts?

I worked from the perspective of "methodological atheism," accepting the central tenet of the sociology of knowledge that religion is to be viewed as a human projection.[41] This means I believe that the way in which religious concepts are symbolized within a particular social order bears marks of human experiences within that social order. But, as Peter Berger has pointed out, this formulation of the sociology of knowledge is incomplete. For it fails to rule out the possibility that "these projected meanings may have an ultimate status independent of man."[42] To assert that religious symbols and meanings are created by human beings, and that they vary according to particular social experiences, is not to eliminate the possibility that they are grounded in "truth." One conducts sociological investigation about religious phenomena as if they were humanly constructed; but that stance may properly include only a suspension, rather than a denial, of religious belief.

And so I have attempted in my analyses to bracket my own religious convictions. Despite the seeming reasonableness of Berger's formulation, however, this has proved difficult. I cannot help but read the sermons from the vantage point of the collective traditions and personal experience of my (non-Christian) faith. I tried, as I worked, to maintain a dialogue between the sermons and the premises of my religious background and convictions, so as at least to make my biases explicit. But of course some biases are so deep-rooted that they have not come to the surface. Equally problematical, I read the sermons from the vantage point of a member of a highly secular culture, working in a secular profession (academics) within its arguably most secular discipline (sociology). Thus, it is likely that much has eluded me on this score, as I simply take for granted assumptions in the sermons without being able to delve more deeply into them.[43]

I do not mean to suggest, however, that the issue of interpretive validity remains unaddressed. In a work of qualitative research such as this, the analyst can take steps to militate against the loss of rigor. There are three general ways in which I have attempted to guard my analyses from idiosyncrasy. First, the theoretical formulations and rhetorical devices that inform my study are identified throughout, and the reader may check whether these ideas and techniques have been responsibly applied to the sermons. Second, the very methodological procedures of the style of discourse analysis I used resist idiosyncrasy, since they require revision of tentative interpretations based on disconfirming cases. Thus, the researcher is forced to construct a larger network of meaningfulness and coherence, in order to tie together analysis of parts of texts.[44] Finally, I reproduce verbatim the sermon excerpts on which my analyses depend, so the reader may assess the adequacy of my interpretations.

To understand the condition of religious speech in contemporary American culture, we must first explore the ways in which religious speakers can respond to secularity. Chapter two sets forth general responses of accommodation, resistance, and reframing gleaned from the theoretical literature and empirical studies.

In chapters three through six, I examine talk about substantive religious and social issues in the sermons. Chapter three explores the variety of images of God, stemming largely from interpretations of the father of the prodigal son. Chapter four concerns the sermons' notions of the secular world, encompassing the social, cultural, and physical worlds alike, which flow from examinations of the dimensions of the far country. Chapter five details the idea of sin, with particular attention given to the use of the rhetorical strategy of civility. And chapter six examines presentations of the nature of the self, highlighting themes of human nature and human need in the context of conversion.

Finally, in chapter seven, I consider the textual analyses comprehensively in light of the theoretical discussion.

Secular Culture and the
Churches' Responses

Since secularity may have a profound effect on the doctrines and ideologies of modern religion, the study of religious language may provide an important new direction for secularization research. Although social scientists have not tended to turn their attention systematically to religious speech, it is possible to glean ideas about the responses religious speakers can make to secular culture from some of their writings. These include the works of those who study religion as a meaning system—especially Peter Berger, James Hunter, and Thomas Luckmann—and others concerned with the role of symbols in religio-cultural expression—Robert Bellah, Mary Douglas, Richard Fenn, George Lindbeck and Robert Wuthnow.[1]

In this chapter, I discuss three general categories of discursive response to secularity: accommodation, resistance, and reframing.[2] In the discussion of accommodation, I also note the social processes that induce religious speakers to adapt their teaching to the norms of the secular world. The three categories are meant to be read as ideal types, of course, none totally characterizing a single concrete case of response. Indeed, as we shall see, the speech of many of the sermons discussed here defies simple categorization, as speakers meld attributes of the three formulations in complex patterns. But the discussion in this chapter should provide a general idea of the possibilities for religious talk within the context of modernity, and of the configuration taken by the talk as it replies to the offerings of the secular world.

Accommodation to the World

Accommodation refers to the adjustments that religion makes in its practices, pronouncements, and creeds to bring them in conformity with the values and behavior of secularity. According to sociologists who have examined the shifts in practices and beliefs of Western religious groups over time, three social processes in modern culture have been the most influential in prompting responses of accommodation. These are closely related movements toward privatization, pluralization, and rationalization.[3]

Privatization and Accommodation

Privatization refers to the shrinking sphere of plausibility of religion in the modern world, as religious explanations are rendered increasingly irrelevant. The social world of the modern West has been differentiated into domains of public and private life. As bureaucratic institutions have come to dominate the public sphere, the rational practices by which they operate have mooted religious explanations and procedures from application to public life. As a result, the only social space remaining to religious relevance is the private sphere, the domain of the individual and her close relationships, such as family and friends.[4]

The migration of religion from the public to the private sphere has had multiple effects on religious speech. For one thing, it has constricted the scope of topics that religion may legitimately address. As religion is disconnected in the West from the institutional life of the state, the law, and the economy, topics concerning the conduct and goals of these public sphere activities are no longer seriously considered from a strictly religious point of view within the political forum. The public sphere no longer seriously entertains debate *solely on religious grounds* concerning issues of justice or morality (for example, the issues of abortion, the right to die, or acts of civil disobedience aimed at industries of war).[5] Instead, these topics become matters for consideration and adjudication under the aegis of secular institutional bodies, such as panels of medical experts and courts of law, with correspondingly secular discourses brought to bear on debate.[6] Routed from the public sphere, then, religion has nowhere else to go than to consider the private concerns of human beings.

What are the features of privatized religious speech? In his examination of some popular literature by contemporary Christian evangelical writers, James Hunter notes that the religious concerns of the literature tend to emphasize the subjective states of individuals such as feelings and needs. Hunter speculates that the narrowing of the horizon of religious relevance to the private sphere alone enlarges the importance of religion within the single domain of life remaining to it.[7] Likewise, Jürgen Habermas observes that modern religion speaks to the need for personal integration in the fragmented conditions of modernity.[8] As another scholar puts it, modern people "escape" the secularism of the world through "one or another expedition into the alleged depths of human consciousness itself."[9] Religious topics of relevance are those that treat the inner workings of the self as the focus for in-depth analysis, frequently conducted through the secular language of psychology.[10] Such discourses raise, and linger on, psychological issues such as concern with self-awareness, self-exploration, self-knowledge, and self-expression.[11]

In this speech, some elements of traditional religious language are meshed with the popular psychological vocabulary of humanistic therapy, emphasizing notions of personal "authenticity," "actualizing one's potential," "growing and developing," and "overcoming defenses." One indicator of the strength of this mixed speech register is the recent birth of an entire publishing classification, that of "Christian psychology." Books published under this classification carry such titles as, *From Bondage to Bonding: Escaping Codependency, Embracing Biblical Love* and *If I'm Forgiven, Why Do I Feel So Guilty?*

Another indication of the privatization of religious speech is its emphasis on practical rationality. By this I mean, following Max Weber, the interest in working out the routine affairs of everyday life in the most expedient manner.[12] Religious speech is concerned with the pragmatic issues of doing things in everyday life, so much so that spirituality may take a back seat to pragmatism. This language highlights such matters as coping with depression and doubt, gaining peace of mind and self-respect, achieving success on the job, and relating well to one's children and/or parents. Christian self-help books, such as *Becoming a Whole Person in a Broken World* and *How to Be a Hero to Your Kids*, are prominent examples of this genre, which arose in the 1940s and 1950s with the publication of Norman Vincent Peale's *The Power of Positive Thinking* and Joshua Loth Liebman's *Peace of Mind*.[13]

The focus on inner states also invites speech oriented largely to the present—to "natural" life, life on earth. Concern with the pragmatic business of life stands to diminish attention to affairs of the "hereafter." Coupled with cultural forces that deemphasize notions of divine punishment for wrongdoing, the "now" orientation reduces the strength of talk about sin and its consequences. For example, James Hunter found that evangelicals are advised to softpedal notions of hell and damnation in their discussions with potential converts.[14] Cultural commentators, such as Karl Menninger, have noted an overall diminution of the notion of sin in modern American religion.[15] And while the majority of the respondents in a recent replication of the famous Middletown study said that they believed in "heaven," few were able to attach specific meaning or images to that concept.[16]

Privatization also affects religious ideology through its tendency to separate religious tenets from one another. As religion becomes increasingly privatized, adherents may decide not to accept the creeds or doctrines of their church as a "package deal." Instead, they may exercise their freedom to pick and choose among church teachings, professing and following some and denying the importance or the relevance of others.[17] This tendency appears widespread among Roman Catholics in the United States, for example, who may reject teachings against contraception at the same time as they accept other church doctrines and pronouncements. An extreme formulation is the case of "Sheilaism," a private religion invented by one of the interview subjects cited in *Habits of the Heart*: The tenets of Sheila's faith consist of the messages of "her own little voice."[18] As Peter Berger notes, because of the loss of collective identity that such individuation entails, adherents find it difficult to maintain their versions of these faiths and easily alter or abandon them.[19]

Pluralization and Accommodation

Pluralization refers to the proliferation of socially legitimated ideologies in the West. The retreat of religion from the public sphere has been accompanied by a massive deinstitutionalization of religious belief and practice. The state has lost its power to constitute a single religious ideology or institution as official. No public body, including the state, has enforcement rights over the religious behavior of citizens. As a result, religion is demonopolized and loses its ability to compel participation; the field is thus open to multiple religious ideologies competing for the allegiance of potential adherents.[20]

This development has been abetted by the social forces of cultural diversity, including urbanization and the growth of the mass media. As life in cities forces subcultures into close proximity with one another, and as television, radio, films, and newspapers portray divergent lifestyles, people come into close contact with belief systems and ways of life other than those to which their group traditionally has adhered.[21] As individuals are relatively freed to choose their religious affiliation, a condition arises which is much like that of an open market. Religious bodies vie with one another for adherents, selling themselves as if they were commodities. In addition to competing with one another, religious organizations contend with overarching secular worldviews for adherents. These worldviews—which offer a coherent, unified vision of life, much as does religion—include quasi-religious formulations such as Marxism, humanism, scientism, and even, most recently, the cult of physical perfectionism.[22]

The constitution of religion as a market commodity by the forces of pluralism has important implications for religious speech. First, it drives churches to supply potential adherents—who are, in effect, comparison shoppers—with specific inducements to participate in one religious body rather than another, or in none at all.[23] As might be expected, these inducements are based on the promise of benefits rather than on explicit or implicit threats for noncompliance. The deinstitutionalization of religion, and the accompanying deobjectication of faith, make it difficult for any religion or denomination to claim a monopoly on truth. Therefore, threats that one will miss out on the chance for salvation and be punished in the afterlife if one does not adhere to a particular version of religion, lack plausibility in the modern context.

Because of the strain toward pragmatism and "this-worldly" concerns that I have already discussed, positive inducements are likely to appear in the form of arguments to utility: religious pronouncements that address the individual practitioner's assumed question, "What's in it for me?" The burden of the argument rests on the church to justify its pragmatic benefit to the would-be adherent. In materials soliciting potential members, for example, churches are apt to advertise participation as "enjoyable," by dint of "exciting music," "uplifting messages" and the opportunity to socialize with friendly people. The moral and spiritual demands that religion places on adherents tend to be underplayed or explicitly denied. (As Robert Schuller wrote recently: "The Ten Commandments are meant—not to take the fun out of life—but to turn on the sun in our life.")[24] The idea of divine punishment and retribution for sin diminishes in importance within Christian speech; instead, emphasis is placed on the emotional and material pleasures said to follow from Christian practice and belief.

A second way in which the market status of religion may affect its speech is to move religious pronouncements closer to secular ideologies. Theorists speculate that since most potential "consumers" of religion spend their everyday lives in a fully secular context, religious ideologies that lean too far in the direction of supernaturalism will appear contradictory to their routine experiences and will therefore be unacceptable.[25] Thus, we see the tendency to demythologize religion, to soften or eliminate its traditionally supernatural content. This can take the form of omitting references to less commonly accepted spiritual entities such as the Devil, of giving explanations for putatively supernatural phenomena in natural vocabularies of common sense or psychology, and of stressing the human, as opposed to the supernatural, character of the Christian God. The academic discourses of anthropology, history, philology, and comparative religion are invoked to make theological points.[26]

A related outcome, in a pluralistic world in which there is no clear right and wrong belief, is an increase in civility. Toleration of others' beliefs is stressed, and points of similarity or relatedness between one's own faith and that of others is highlighted. Care is taken, particularly with respect to potentially touchy issues, to couch one's language so as to send out the message, "no offense."[27]

These tendencies strain traditional ideas of denominational identity. Combined with the effects of rationalization, the availability of various competing religious options simultaneously loosens and tightens denominational self-definition. On the one hand, church organizations are forced toward isomorphism: In terms of their structures and their teachings, denominations increasingly come to resemble one another.[28] Thus, the symbolic boundaries between one denomination and another weaken, and it may be hard to ascertain, for example, exactly how "Presbyterians" differentiate themselves from "Methodists." On the other hand, the market forces at work under conditions of pluralism demand that there be at least some marginal degree of differentiation among the creeds and practices of denominations, so that potential adherents have some reason to choose one over the next.[29]

Rationalization and Accommodation

Rationalization, a third element of secularity, entails the growth of practices in various areas of life that calculate the efficiency or effectiveness of alternative means to a given end.[30] Some of the possible effects of rationalization on religious speech have already been discussed, since they are linked to privatization and pluralization. These include an emphasis on handling the affairs of everyday life, a focus on positive inducements for religious affiliation, and explanations of religious phenomena in secular terms of psychology or common sense. We should, however, also note the impact of rationalization on the formal structures of religious creeds and procedures. For example, James Hunter observes the degree to which prescriptions concerning spirituality are standardized and made methodical in evangelical texts.[31] In these texts, behavioral precepts are organized in a series of steps, or items on a list, which call for the reader's systematic compliance; one's progress toward spirituality is thus measured on an ascending scale. In addition, the form of this talk mirrors its popular, secular counterpart, the "how-to" book. The talk may be framed as a series of self-referring, self-justifying, rules, "steps," or "principles," adherence to which induces personal growth and fulfillment. Taken to the extreme, this talk constitutes a "do-it-yourself" guide for personal satisfaction, with a few mentions of God or faith or prayer tossed in to mark itself as "religious."

Another element of standardization involves simplification of religious pronouncements. James Hunter discusses the presentation of doctrine in his sample of evangelical texts in terms of "packaging." Tenets of faith and behavior are smoothed into easily "consumable" forms, omitting complicating details or contingencies.[32] Generalization and systematization turn doctrines into mass-market commodities, easily comprehended and adopted by broad constituencies. For example, some researchers have noted the tendency of popular Christian speech to conflate the once-specific qualities of the persons of the Trinity into a general characterization of "God," and, further, to reduce qualities of the deity into terms most amenable to straightforward understanding.[33] Simplification is apparent, too, in the trend toward Bible translations into "everyday English" and "ordinary language" versions of traditional liturgies.[34]

Resistance to Secular Culture

The devices of language I label accommodation to today's secular culture are not the only resources for modern Protestantism. The group of strategies I call resistance is associated, in its most marked forms within contemporary American Protestantism, with fundamentalist and some evangelical reactions to the modern world. I discuss only the most extreme case of fundamentalist resistance here—and an ideal type of the resistance, at that—as illustration of the discursive techniques that other, more moderate, reactions against secular culture may use in part as they attempt to buffer religion from the pressures of modernity.

The fundamentalist movement germinated after the First World War in the context of a growing theological liberalism within Protestantism. Fundamentalism was self-consciously conceived as an attempt to protect central tenets of conservative Christianity, such as biblical inerrancy, from the onslaught of relativizing developments within biblical criticism and from the Darwinian theory of evolution. The movement drew some of its themes from arguments set forth in a set of books published between 1910 and 1913, called *The Fundamentals*. They included points concerning the inerrancy of Scripture, the virgin birth of Jesus, the belief that Jesus died for the sins of humankind, the notion that Jesus was physically resurrected from the dead, and the doctrine of the second coming.[35] With minor modifications, these doctrines have remained the hallmark of contemporary conservative Protestantism, including the dominant faction of the Southern Baptist Convention.

Fundamentalism is popularly caricatured as an anti-intellectual, emotion-filled backlash against modernity. This image has been fueled by Richard Hofstadter's influential characterization of fundamentalism as a populist upsurge against academic science, a manifestation of "a new kind of popular mind: 100-percentism, tolerating no ambiguities, equivocations, reservations, or criticisms." In this acerbic view, fundamentalists were mounting a rearguard attack against "everything modern—higher criticism, evolution, the social gospel, rational criticism of any kind."[36] The result, Hofstadter wrote, was a folkish, mindless conservatism at war against any variety of progressive liberalism.

While Hofstadter's interpretation—and that of other equally harsh contemporary commentators on fundamentalism—may accurately describe some of the more florid segments of the movement, other scholars, who allow fundamentalists to speak with their own voices, help us gain a more balanced picture of their revolt.[37] Through these writings, we are able to look more objectively at the form and content of fundamentalist resistance to the secularization of religious thought.

As fundamentalism's more even-minded commentators make clear, fundamentalist resistance rests not on emotion or irrationalism (although it is accurate to call it "anti-intellectual") but on the cornerstone of Baconian thought and Scottish Common Sense Realism, which characterized much of the intellectual base of science in the United States from the founding of the republic through much of the nineteenth century.[38] Under the tenets of Baconian science, the world as created by God conforms to an orderly system of laws, graspable through the mechanisms of careful commonsense observation. The role of the scientist is to observe phenomena, classify data gleaned from observation, and make generalizations closely derived from the data. Just so, Scripture is to be viewed as a collection of facts that reflect natural and supernatural realities (indeed, in some variants of fundamentalist thought, Scripture contains *all* the information that can be called "factual"). Scripture should be read according to the same scientific procedures: gleaning data (the text) and interpreting the text through plain sense. In this view, Scripture is a record of the truth, to be read literally wherever possible; the truths it contains are not obscure, allegorical, or in need of deep interpretation.

Looked at in terms of language use, the heart of fundamentalist resistance contains two linked movements: resacralization, or reinserting elements of the sacred into contexts where it had been diluted by liberalism; and constructing religious arguments so that they are formally seamless and cohesive. Both movements are intimately concerned with claims about the nature of truth and the source of guarantees for these claims. Together, these movements lead to a third: setting clear symbolic boundaries to segregate truth from error, the faithful from the faithless.

As a defense against the relativism of modern culture—for example, the challenges to certainty launched by modern science, especially by the theory of relativity;[39] the pluralistic orientations of social science; and the breakdown of strict standards in public displays of morality—fundamentalists resacralize the world by positing a universe of assured, unchanging fact, based on the guarantees of supernatural revelation. This revelation is not a gnosis, a set of mysterious truths available only to a select group of initiates. Instead, the core premise of fundamentalism is that the details of the one universal and eternal truth are openly contained in the form of Scripture, available to everyone willing to read or hear it as the inerrant word of God. No special training or expertise is needed to understand the truth as it appears in the Bible: It rests on the face of things—clear, plain, and a matter of common sense.[40]

In essence, fundamentalist resacralization involves resistance to the possibility of multiple, competing sources of authority. In practice, this works itself out as a claim concerning a single, total, source of truth (Scripture); a single guarantee for that claim (that it is God's word); and a single meaning of the claim (literal, plain sense reading).[41] This is the sense in which Scripture is said to be inerrant and infallible—*inerrant,* meaning that there can be no mistake in the original document of Scripture; *infallible*, meaning that Scripture cannot escape God's intended purpose for it. One can see how this approach "solves" the problems created by the encroachment of secularity on religion. It resacralizes religion by removing its pronouncements from the realm of human interpretation, which might give rise to all sorts of variant readings; Scripture is not what men and women make of it but, rather, what God literally says through it. If it is God who speaks—a God with a single, clear purpose for humankind—the possibility of multiple meanings is ruled out and issues of interpretation are made moot. With this source of authority at its core, fundamentalism attempts to eliminate the ambiguities that characterize modern secular culture.

Not only is Scripture inerrant and infallible, in this view; it is also completely coherent. By this, fundamentalists mean that every part of Scripture is clearly and logically connected with every other part; each verse of the Bible gives evidence for and sheds light on every other verse. The practice of prooftexting—supporting truth claims based on Scripture with related scriptural citations—sustains the reading of the Bible as coherent and complete.[42] Like the assertion of inerrancy, coherence serves to rule out the possibility of alternative readings. It works by buffering each important truth claim from disconfirmation because it is logically required by every other central truth claim. Because the core tenets of faith are coupled so tightly, it is difficult for adherents to pick and choose from among the few key fundamentalist doctrines; one doctrine logically entails the other. Thus fundamentalism militates against the religious fragmentation and relativism that occur as part of the accommodative response to modernity.

Because Scripture is deemed the source of truth about doctrinal claims, fundamentalists believe it is also a reliable guide to issues of morality and lifestyle. Behavioral prescriptions and taboos are commonly defended on the basis of their "t" with biblical scripts, even when the issues at hand are not addressed in the Bible.[43] Grounding precepts, no matter how seemingly "nonreligious," in Scripture, not only lends these precepts coherence, but also gives them a high degree of seriousness. Thus, matters like the ordination of women, feminist political issues like support for the Equal Rights Amendment, the use of alcohol, and even dancing, movie attendance, and television watching, can be condemned as unscriptural with the same degree of force and certainty as more apparently theological issues such as homosexuality or abortion.

27

The firm basis of doctrinal tenets and their close interconnection allow for another rhetorical device of resistance: the sealing of symbolic boundaries between spheres of correct and erroneous doctrine and between populations who inhabit the spheres. The lines of demarcation are drawn as if apparent and immutable; categories of "us" and "other" are clearly circumscribed. The extreme fundamentalist doctrine of separation both entails and strengthens this rhetorical structure. The doctrine insures that unbelievers will be grouped together in one undifferentiated category—a total rejection, not only of modernist relativism, but also even the premise of pluralism. And further, it assures that believers will be protected from contact with the force of unbelievers' "sinful" conduct and meanings.

Taken together, the resacralization of the world based on a sole reliance on Scripture, the construction of coherence around core claims, and the protection of adherents from alternative interpretations erect a barricade between the resistant community and the battering rams of modern secular culture.

REFRAMING OF RELIGIOUS ISSUES

Both sets of responses we have examined so far, antithetical as they may be to each other in their approach to modernity, have a central assumption in common: that religious speech appropriately offers arguments and makes claims about truth. Speech may have other, subsidiary functions. For example, it may express and dramatize the sincerity of one's conversion experience, or bind practitioners together through the performance of a liturgy, or constitute the authority of the speaker. But at the core, as the basis for other types of speech claims, is the idea that utterances about doctrine refer to objective phenomena beyond the words themselves. In this view, the underlying purpose of religious speech is to reflect a reality that is "out there," grounded in objective truth.

As some theorists have suggested, there may be a third type of responsive strategy available to contemporary religious speakers, which I have termed reframing. This strategy arises from a broad intellectual movement in which language is viewed not primarily as a vehicle for reflecting reality, but as a means for *creating* it.[44] As speakers reframe religious issues, they reconceive the primary function of religious speech away from rendering propositional claims (such as, "Jesus died for our sins" or "You must be born again to be saved"). Instead, speakers use religious formulations principally to provide holistic meaning, on two levels: to people as individuals, by supplying overarching significance to the whole of life; and to people as members of collectivities, by orienting them around shared symbols in community.

One hallmark of religion in modern societies, writes the sociologist Robert Bellah, is a heightened self-consciousness about the role symbols play in religious culture.[45] Modern men and women sense that religious symbols have important functions other than that of referring to a set of supernatural truths. They feel that, in addition, the symbols themselves are available for use in order to make meanings. In effect, this belief about the dual role of symbolism makes possible a type of compartmentalization. On the one hand are the transcendent truths that the symbols have traditionally conveyed, which many modern people may not accept. But on the other hand are the symbols themselves, still resonant with significance even within a secular context, which can be used to construct a set of ultimate meanings for humankind. For example, for some contemporary Christians, the symbol of the cross may no longer plausibly refer to the accounts of the crucifixion and resurrection of Jesus as they appear in the gospels. Yet the cross may take on significance in another way as speakers use it to condense and dramatize notions of suffering and its transcendence, or overwhelming love, or the possibilities of human transfiguration.

Now I think it is correct to view the separation of symbol from traditional referent as a device of accommodation in its own right. It reduces the likelihood of supernatural interpretations, since it does away with the need to refer to some transcendent truth. It invites the opportunity for multiple interpretations of the same symbol, diminishing the force of corporately held dogmas and creeds. But the accommodation is not complete, since the separation of symbol from traditional referent salvages the symbols themselves for use for serious and authentically religious purposes. It allows men and women to draw on the resonance of the symbols to create statements about the meaning of the whole of life.[46] It serves, if not to buffer traditional creeds from the effects of secularity, at least to protect the symbols themselves.

Thus reoriented, what can religious symbols do? If the symbols are no longer constrained to play under the rules of the losing game, in the modern context, that they must reflect external truths, yet if they are

29

still able to signify something centrally meaningful about human existence, then they are freed to become metacommunication, or communication about communication: to serve as overarching themes to help give meaning to all of one's life. In this view, religious symbols can be used to interpret the discourses of other realms—the realms of external science, of internal phenomenology, of intersubjective experience, that are so differentiated and fragmented within the culture of modernity— and to integrate these spheres of meaning into a unified whole for the individual. In this understanding, the assumptions of the traditional objectivist view of religion are reversed: Instead of propositional truths giving meaning to religion, it is religion that gives meaning to the propositional truths of other realms.

So far, I have focused on the potential functions of reframing at the level of the individual. But these notions also suggest a powerful role for religious symbols in shaping communities. Even though religion may no longer be viewed as referring to transcendent truths (which, in some traditional views of religion, serve to collect and connect the community as the individual is subsumed to the whole), yet there is another possible overarching point of convergence, one of at least partial integration. For as religious practitioners orient around religious symbols and *simultaneously recognize the socially constructed nature of meaning,* as they are aware that, singly and collectively, they create the significations that these symbols have for them, they are bound together even so in the relations and obligations of the larger social order. The making of meaning is a serious business. It is fraught with issues of authority, of justice, and of moral responsibility, as many contemporary religious practitioners, struggling over issues of inclusiveness and fairness, well know. And the gravity of the task underscores the centrality of religion to human life, to individuals and collectivities alike, even if religion may no longer lay claim to reflecting and recording the truth.

CHAPTER THREE

God as Daddy, Sufferer, Lover, and Judge

God and man are two qualities between which there is an
infinite qualitative difference. Every doctrine which
overlooks this difference is, humanly speaking,
crazy; understood in a godly sense,
it is blasphemy.
(Soren Kierkegaard, *Sickness unto Death*)

Affirm OUT LOUD: ' I am God's friend. God loves me.
If God has chosen me for His friend,
I must be a marvelous person.'
(Robert Schuller, *Believe in the God Who Believes in You*)

F ROM THE LOOKS of survey data, contemporary Protestant belief in the United States is blossoming in the nutrients of spiritual soil. Today's Americans overwhelmingly profess the importance of God in their lives. Recent Gallup polls indicate that 94 percent of Americans say they believe in God, 90 percent say they pray to God, and three quarters say they think deeply about their relationship to God. Nine in ten Americans say they have never even doubted the existence of God. More than three quarters say they are sharply conscious of the presence of God in their daily affairs. And a third of Americans indicate that they have had, at one time or another, a mystical feeling of unity with God.[1]

Especially when compared with similar data about the religious beliefs of Britons, or the French, or people living in other Western democracies, these statistics are remarkable.[2] In the face of the high degree of scientific and technological development in the United States, a formally secular political system, a tradition of individualism and self-reliance, and a high standard of living—all of which might argue against the centrality of religious beliefs—Americans express certainty that God exists and that he works in their lives, both through extraordinary "otherworldly" experiences and in their daily affairs.

But while these data from opinion polls are useful for gauging the degree to which religion is an important category in American thought

31

and practice, a significant question, which cannot be probed by these surveys, has remained largely ignored. Exactly who *is* God for contemporary American Christians? In what image has he been created? What are the qualities of this deity to whom people pray, of whose effects in their lives they are aware, whose guidance they trust? How do contemporary ideas of God square with the influence of rationality, the dominance of ideologies of science and technology, widespread notions of individual autonomy, the acknowledgment and even acceptance of diversity—all of which characterize life for the vast majority of twentieth-century Americans?

Repertoires of Speaking about God

Since its beginning, Protestant theology has made recourse to two vocabularies about the deity, those concerning the "transcendent" and the "immanent" aspects of God. Together, these vocabularies describe the Christian notion of God's double nature. In the most radical formulation of his transcendent aspect, God is "wholly other"—inscrutable to people, indescribable in terms of human qualities, utterly different from human beings.

To speak correctly about God, one must use the indirection of the *via negationis*, a theological formulation which says that all we can say about God, all that is knowable about God, is that which God is not. When this formulation is partially weakened by anthropomorphization, God in his transcendent aspect is portrayed partly through the human metaphors of "sovereign" and "judge." He is Lord of all. He dispenses punishment to those who disobey him. His range and capabilities are complete and terrible. The metaphors are not sufficient to capture his omnipotence, however. It is not possible fully for human beings to understand God's behavior, much less predict with certainty what he will do. Not even the righteous can count on his blessings. This is the God of Exodus 3:14, who tells Moses, "I am that I am." People are not meant to know him, to be familiar with him, to address him in human terms. The appropriate stance before the Lord of Hosts is humility, self-abasement, and awe.

But the harshness of God's transcendence is countered by his immanent presence. God acts by inserting himself in human history. His judgment is admixed with mercy; he is primarily a beneficent force in human affairs. God loves his people, his creation; so much so that he took on human form to effect his plan of redemption.

As these double discourses about God have taken concrete form within American Protestantism, new nuances have been lent to their shape and meaning. The Calvinist roots of religious practice in Colonial America—with Calvinism's emphasis on the transcendent and inscrutable God of judgment—were confronted with unsettling challenges by social and cultural developments in the nineteenth century. Popular ideologies of voluntarism, democratism, and pragmatism suffused political ideals and concrete forms of social organization.[3] These ideologies contributed new repertoires of religious speech to the "God-talk" of ordinary Americans, mitigating the harsh Calvinist doctrine of predestination and suggesting that human beings can, in fact, contribute to their own salvation. In addition, the restless impulse of evangelicalism that marked nearly all of the nineteenth century in the United States underscored notions of the accessibility of God to human beings, both through personal (often affective) experience of God and through individual competence to read and interpret Scripture.[4] Developments in the late nineteenth and early twentieth centuries contributed the notions of optimism about human nature and the ineluctable march of human progress, both of which deemphasized sinfulness (and thus, God's judgmental face) and constructed further bridges to the divine through an enriched vocabulary of immanence.[5]

Yet these challenges to doctrines of the transcendent nature of God themselves met with resistance from various factions of Protestantism. In the mid-1800s, conservative Presbyterian clergy and theologians and practitioners of other Reformed movements criticized the excesses of revivalism. They decried its overwhelming emphasis on human affect and other aspects of subjectivity, and on notions of human voluntarism with respect to salvation, urging a return to definitions of religious practice centered upon the power of a majestic God.[6] In the twentieth century, both fundamentalism and neo-orthodoxy countered liberal optimism and human-centered theologies with reassertion of the doctrine of the fallen nature of human beings and with the image of a mighty God who is "angry about sin." Neo-orthodoxy, in particular, underscored the separation between God and humankind by positing a majestically transcendent God whose distance from human beings is incalculable and unbridgeable and who resists human efforts to know and understand him.[7] To a far lesser extent, some elements of evangelicalism in the twentieth century have also conceived of a God who waits in judgment over those who depart from his will, although the major categories of evangelical talk about God tend to emphasize one's personal experience of an immanent deity.[8]

Thus, the pendulum has remained in motion over the years of the American Protestant experience—now favoring, now rejecting, the predominant imagery of a transcendent God. Both vocabularies, those of transcendence and immanence, remain available as resources of speech to practitioners of Protestantism in the late twentieth century. What about contemporary "God-talk" in the Protestant churches? How does today's speech about the deity use ideas about the dual aspects of God in seeking to deal with the challenges of modern times for religious speech?

Although the theoretical speculation has been considerable, the empirical evidence is thin.[9] Most suggestive is James Hunter's discussion of the language of popular evangelical texts of the 1970s and 80s.[10] In these works, the traditional transcendent imagery concerning God has been minimized in favor of emphasis on depictions of some of God's immanent features: his benevolence, love, and sympathy for humankind. Easily accessible, God is patiently concerned with the extraordinary and daily problems of people. He is tolerant of human foibles and errors, and democratic in his treatment of mortal beings. When God is seen in transcendent terms at all, his fearsome qualities are either deemphasized or banished from the discourse and replaced by portraits of a clear-thinking, well-organized "super-administrator," one of whose primary functions is to plan efficiently the affairs of the universe.

What can the sermons from the two denominations tell us about contemporary speech about God? I first turn to a general examination of the qualities of God that appear in the sermons.

General Characterizations of God

The sermons provide evidence that talk about God continues to be an important concern in the teachings of the two denominations under study here. In thirty-one sermons, or two-thirds of the total, God is centrally present—as the locus of orientation around which the action revolves, the focal point for teaching and presenting moral messages, and the motivation for teaching the parable. While the human self is of abiding concern to many of the pastors, as we shall see in chapter six, in these sermons the nature of the self stems from the nature of God; to that extent, at least, the sermons retain a central place for utterances about the supernatural.

Yet the focus of concerns that these sermons articulate about God is extremely narrow. In the great majority (82 percent of the sermons that centrally concern God), God is portrayed exclusively or predominantly in terms of the positive functions he serves for men and women.[11] Chief among these functions is one that can be labeled "therapeutic." God relieves negative feelings, especially anxiety and doubt. In this speech, God usually is assigned the qualities of generosity, exceptional loving-ness, accessibility, and patience. In addition, emphasis is placed on God's inner psychological states, especially on his feelings, which, in part, serve to render him familiarly human. As we shall see, these qual-ities are displayed and dramatized through two categories of speech: "God as daddy" and "God as sufferer."

A third category of speaking about God, which appears in some Presbyterian sermons, supplies a certain counterdiscourse to the first two categories, although it is only partial and sometimes quite tenta-tive. In these depictions, although God still is characterized by his im-manent qualities, especially the instrumental functions of his love and concern for humankind, the sermons hint at ways in which God's na-ture cannot be encapsulated within human terms. God fulfills functions of comfort and forgiveness for human beings, just as he does in the first two sets of sermons. But here the point is made—or more frequently, adumbrated—that God's actions are inexplicable within a human vo-cabulary. Instead of the self-interest that characterizes mortal behavior, God is impelled by love to sacrifice himself on the cross. Instead of dealing with human beings as they do with one another, through the rational calculus of instrumentalism and exchange, God operates ac-cording to a mysterious and a-rational norm of forgiveness. These ideas are articulated within a speech category that can be called "God as extravagant lover."

Another form of counterdiscourse is found in some of the Southern Baptist sermons. Here, various notions of God's transcendent aspects are retained, albeit somewhat softened. While God is loving and merci-ful, he also must be attended to ("feared" is perhaps too strong a word) as the ultimate judge of souls. Whereas God freely forgives the repen-tant, judgment will follow upon those who refuse to change their ways and admit their sin. In this talk, the speech repertoires of God's benevolence for mankind and the majesty of his judgment are intermingled, although God's fearsome qualities are not explicitly articulated. This category may be termed, "God as judge."

Before turning to the analysis, it is important to note that, when the sermons speak of God, they rarely differentiate between "God the Father" and "Jesus Christ." Instead, the term "God" is used to refer to any Person of the Christian Trinity. Thus, the qualities assigned to "God" in this speech are used indiscriminantly to refer to "Jesus Christ" and "God the Father" alike.[12]

GOD THE DADDY

The category of God as daddy occurs in 32 percent of the texts that centrally concern God, only slightly more among Presbyterians than Southern Baptists.[13] In these representations, God is spoken of as standing at the head of his "family" of human children, not in divine majesty but in domestic familiarity, with his tie loosened and his shirt sleeves rolled up. He is a figure of friendship and comfort, a soothing mature presence, available at a moment's notice to those who call on him. As one preacher puts it:[14]

> William Franklin writes these words, "If he's wealthy and prominent and you stand in awe of him, then you call him 'Father.' If he sits in shirt sleeves and suspenders at a ball game and a picnic, then you call him 'Pop.' If he wheels the baby carriage and carries the little one gently, call him 'Papa.' But when he makes a pal of you and becomes your friend, and yet is too wise for you to pull the wool over his loving eyes . . . then you call him 'Dad.' " [P]

God as daddy is thus a friend, a buddy, a constantly accessible companion. But he serves an even more basic function—nurturing his children. Some of the sermons refer to the Aramaic/Hebrew word *Abba* (often translated as "daddy"), which Jesus uses just once in the gospels, to suggest the nurturing role that this God/daddy fulfills.[15] As one pastor preaches:

> Jesus took seriously this very special relationship he had with God as his Father and called all people to trust him as their father as well. To do this Jesus used a strange little word—the word was "ABBA. " . . . It was a babbling sound—the first word that a tiny infant would utter in

relation to his father and mother. . . . This would be equivalent to our baby saying, "DaDa" or "MaMa." You see, "Abba" is a very intimate word between child and parent, between child and father. It conveys all of the oneness and security and trust that exists between an infant and its parents. [SB]

Here, the relationship between a human being and God is presented as the dependence of a helpless infant on its devoted parent. In their explication of the parable, the sermons frequently draw this meaning from the prodigal son's return home: The reunification of the young man with his father is read almost literally as the re-enmeshment of the human being—the child of God—with his heavenly daddy, enveloped in the blanket of his love. The imagery of infancy—of the baby swathed in the blissful security of his comforter, in the warmth of a parent's embrace—is startlingly transparent. As this speaker preaches:

The moral of the [Parable of the Prodigal Son] is as clear as its outcome. When you have done wrong and you know it, you don't have to come crawling back to God. All you have to do, someone said, is to stop running from Him long enough to let Him reach out and gather you safely in His arms. [P]

The safety and security of one's placement in God's arms are paramount themes in some of the sermons. Underlying their speech about God as daddy, and occasionally articulated expressly as its motivation, is the anxiety that these pastors construct in their talk to characterize the human condition. The human psyche is portrayed as beset with insecurity and uncertainty. Consonant with the emphasis in these sermons on the concerns of selfhood, it is the individual person who, alone and without the aid of a human community, confronts anxieties about loneliness and self-worth. And overwhelmingly, it is not the human community but God who relieves these negative feelings, who gives assurances of membership, affiliation and love, who gives assurances of worthiness. One pastor hammers this point home through elaborative detail about the nature of God's love:

God's love has no strings attached to it. It cannot be earned. It cannot be shut off, deterred. It cannot be escaped. God loves us as we are. God loves us for what we are and in spite of what we are. There is nothing we can do to make God love us less. God loves us when no one else does. God loves us when we are unlovable. God loves us when we cannot stand ourselves. [P]

Here, God relieves the anguish of negative feelings in two ways. His unconditional, parentally intimate love for humankind guarantees an attachment, an acceptance, a satisfying relationship even when human relationships fail ("God loves us when no one else does"). In effect, this is the guarantee that, psychologically, one will not be alone; that there will always be someone "there" for us. In addition, God's love helps people overcome self-criticism and transcend feelings of inadequacy ("God loves us when we cannot stand ourselves"). It is a relief from the judgment of self that comes from within: the psychological torment of guilt and self-blame. A preacher expresses the removal of the burden of worry about one's belonging in this way:

> One personal joy in my life, is to experience God's amazing grace extended to all my blunders—to discover that in spite of them, my membership in the family is never in jeopardy. [P]

Another pastor preaches:

> God continues to wait expectantly for us to come to our senses and grow into new levels of love relationships. He waits patiently for us to recognize our need for his help with all the messes into which we've gotten ourselves. [P]

Further stressing the guarantee of belonging given by God's daddy role, a third pastor asks:

> How can I make it clear to you . . . that Christ died on the cross so you could receive unconditional membership in His Forever Family? You don't have to measure up or earn anything! Membership cannot be earned! [P]

There is another source of potential anxiety, too, one which some pastors reveal as they extensively elaborate their idea of the one, correct, fully adequate nature of God. Their strenuous opposition to the image of God as wholly transcendent, in his Old Testament guise of Yahweh—the angry, temperamental, and potentially punitive God—suggests that this is a matter of no small concern. It is not only that God is portrayed predominantly here through his immanent and familiar aspects as daddy; it is that the picture of God in his transcendent role as awesome sovereign and judge is laboriously debunked. The two images are treated as if categorically incompatible with each other; the God who is motivated by nurturing love cannot, even in other circumstances, castigate and judge. One must not be fearful of God, the speakers reassure their listeners, for the picture of God that provokes worry and anxiety is incorrect in its every detail.

In an exposition that draws the contrast by combining comic and Gothic depictions of Yahweh, one preacher says:

> I realize even today as in Jesus' day there are those who want to keep God far, far away. They purposely want him to be a million light years away. They want to speak of him as being senile, old fashioned, and a little deaf. There are other folks who want him to be a father image as they know a father. The kind who terrorizes the family during the middle of the night and threatens to kill them all. Listen! Are you listening! When Jesus called God "father" in the word of "Abba," that was not a term which denoted fear, vindictiveness or terror, it was a word which beautifully described God as "DaDa"; one who loves, one who wants his children to trust him and follow his teachings. [SB]

Another preacher represents this distinction as a categorical dichotomy:

> Out of my past came the harsh image of an angry revival preacher thundering out his message from God: "You're Lost!" Somehow, sometime later this image was changed and as it was changed, I was changed by it. I heard Jesus Christ saying to me, "You're Found." [SB]

A Presbyterian preacher frames the matter even more pithily:

> That's what God is saying to you. It's not "Go to your room." It's "Come to the party!" [P]

And another sermon elaborates:

> Perhaps all of us can cease to see ourselves as sinners in the hands of an angry God and know we are children held in the arms of a loving Father—a Father who seeks to throw a party in our honor. [P]

The complete denial of God's aspect as a wrathful judge makes sense within the context of the need for religion to "market" itself, placing emphasis on the positive rewards, as opposed to the challenges and responsibilities, of faith. As we have seen, some of those rewards entail immediate, unlimited access to God's nurturing and therapeutic functions: a daddy to shelter one from the confusions of the world, to repair one's hurts, and to listen to one's problems. To minimize even further the distance between God and human beings—to hammer home the notion of God's accessibility—many of the sermons present God in almost fully human terms, particularly with respect to his "feelings."

GOD THE SUFFERER

As we have noted, of the several strands that underlie the presentation of God as daddy, one of the most marked is that which renders the divine in terms of the familiar and accessible. That is, God is depicted through human imagery with little or no qualification.

Closely related is the tendency in a sizable portion of the texts (39 percent of those that centrally concern God) to present God through characterizations of his inner states, with an emphasis on his emotions, which closely resemble those of human beings. In this category, the speech labors to make clear within human terms God's "personality" and his reasons for behavior. God is ascribed a familiar, purely human, vocabulary of motives; in some sermons, even his overwhelming quality of love is rendered as talk about domestic concerns.

Just as the sermons tend to emphasize the subjective concerns of human beings, so they also portray God through descriptions of his subjectivity. God is more likely to "feel" than to "act," to "think" than to "say." God's subjectivity is entirely familiar; the nature of his emotions is understandable within the context of human experience, since they are such common emotions as "anguish" or "hurt," or "happiness" or "joy." God's emotions differ from those of human beings solely with respect to their magnitude and, for the positive emotions of love and joy, with respect to the largess with which they are experienced.

Further, God's feelings and inner thoughts are accessible to people. God is rendered here as if he were unreservedly open about his feelings. Just as many of the sermons urge human beings to display themselves to God, in honesty and vulnerability, so God is portrayed as self-revealing and transparent; he would rank high on a psychological scale of self-disclosure. For example, the emotional experiences of some of the human characters in the Parable of the Prodigal Son and the two prior Lucan parables, which are frequently linked in the sermons, are taken to represent almost literally the workings of God in his emotional life. He is without mystery; his inner states are available for human scrutiny and understanding. Just as the removal of the imagery of Yahweh reassures people that they need not fear this God, so the portrayal of God's emotional life attempts to comfort them with the understanding that he is not the Other.

One pastor combines a rejection of the idea of God as Yahweh with a description of his inner feelings. Note that even the debunked portrait of the angry, punitive God carries within it a description of God's internal states:

[A lot of people] feel that God can't wait to get on to them and that every bad thing that happens to them is God's work to punish them for their sins. . . . One can almost get the impression that God secretly anticipates the pronouncement of eternal doom on sinners. The facts are that nothing is further from the truth. No one suffers more anguish over sinners than does God. Rather than desiring judgment, He desires salvation for them. [SB]

The emotional aspects of God are frequently described in vocabulary better suited to the stereotypical imagery of the feminine than to that of the masculine. Instead of language that describes such putatively male responses to sad things as stoicism, silence, squaring of shoulders, or anger, God's reaction to the errant behavior of mortals is portrayed as "anguish" and "hurt feelings." These utterances linger in romantic terms over the portrayal of God's sorrow:

That, in the end, is what the Gospel is all about. A prodigal God, a spendthrift God who spares no expense to let us know He loves us, and who lavishes upon us a wealth of resources in an incredible world, beats us to the punch even, giving us more than we can imagine, before we thought to ask. And who waits for us to come to our senses. If we ever do, before we break His heart. Again. [P]

A second pastor says:

Sin always hurts us and those who care for us! But not only does sin hurt us and those around us, sin is "against heaven." Sin is against God; it breaks the heart of God. For the world and all therein is His. But as the Father received the son, so God receives the confessing sinner. God kisses away the confession even as it's spoken because He loves prodigals. Aren't you glad? [SB]

God's emotions are graphically detailed by another pastor through analogy with the behavior of the father of the prodigal son upon the

41

son's return home. The father's conduct is elaborated in terms so expressive that they cannot be fully stated, only haltingly evoked:

> I wish I could have been there when the son returned—one of the great moments in the New Testament—wet hands—surprise—joy when he felt the forgiving arms of his Father around him—his Father's tears of joy running down his neck. [P]

And another pastor supplies this passage concerning the highly keyed emotional life of the father/God:

> Little did [the prodigal son] know what was going on in his dad's heart. The scripture says that when the boy was still far away, the father saw him. There can be no doubt but that the father had spent many agonizing hours, days, weeks, maybe even years, looking down that road longing for his son to return. [SB]

Some speakers make no distinction between the human behavior of the father and the supposedly supernatural behavior of God in welcoming their errant sons home; the complete conflation of these categories stands out in this excerpt:

> Picture God running to you with outstretched arms. He runs to welcome you home. On your finger he puts a ring kept for a beloved child, and says, "You are my child and that will never change." He puts the robe around you that's kept for special guests. He puts shoes on your feet, a symbol of the fact that you're no longer a slave feeding the swine in the fields. [P]

In detailing God's hurt feelings over human wrongdoing, another pastor analogizes between the feeling states of human fatherhood and those that affect God in his role as parent. We should note the rendering of the truism of contemporary psychology, that to love is to take risks, to be vulnerable to internal pain:

> When God assumed the role of a father he said, "I will be a father unto you," he exposed himself to pain, he made himself vulnerable to pain. Because you cannot be a parent without that. And the greater your capacity to love, the greater your capacity to hurt. [SB]

The most extreme example of exploiting depictions of God's emotional nature is located in the following excerpt from a Southern Baptist sermon. The speaker uses emotional detail to urge listeners not merely to understand God, but to place themselves in his position, in his role as Father:

> Imagine for a moment how God must have felt seeing his son leave home, knowing he must be executed like a criminal for you and me. Jesus was God's favorite and only son. How would you like to see your son leave home knowing that this would happen to him? [SB]

And the sermon later continues:

> Jesus had to die so that we could be forgiven for our sins. The story of the cross becomes so familiar that it loses its meaning to us, but not to God—it cost him His son. If something cost you your son, you wouldn't forget it, would you? [SB]

Quite transparently, this speech is an attempt to evoke feelings of guilt on the part of listeners. If one can demonstrate that God has suffered so in order to fulfill his plan of salvation, the onus is placed on listeners to conform to God's will: "We" made him suffer, and we continue to do so without our repentance. Especially in the context of diminished attention to the penalties for sin in these sermons, the construction of guilt plays a key motivational role in inspiring correct faith and behavior: It is perhaps the only remaining negative inducement. But beyond attempts to engender guilt, the appeal in these utterances achieves another effect. The invitation to listeners to place themselves in God's shoes constitutes a remarkable attempt to forge an identification between human beings and God. Identification is possible because people are able not merely to *speculate* about God's feelings but, indeed, to *empathize* with them. People should be able to imagine what God's suffering feels like, because their loss of a son would feel the same way. They would not wish to lose a son any more than God liked losing his. This reasoning, along with the emotional appeal behind it, makes an unqualified equation of God's inner feelings and those of human beings. Thus, God is not only depicted as an emotional being, but is also rendered as fully transparent with respect to his emotions; human beings can feel exactly the same things.

This example provides the outer limit of the extent to which God has been shorn of his transcendent qualities in the speech of these sermons. Any possible distance between God and humankind is summarily removed. God is presented here through his subjectivity. Human beings are somehow privy to what goes on, unexpressed, "inside God's head." Not only can people decipher God's inner states, but the states are fully rendered here as "feelings." And people are not only shown God's emotions, but are invited actually to participate in them through empathy. Thus there is nothing to stand in the way of an emotional identification with God. Not only is he the throbbing heart at the center of the universe; his heart is man's heart. It is hard to think of imagery further removed from the quotation from Kierkegaard at the beginning of this chapter, or, perhaps even more markedly, from the emblematic description of God's transcendence supplied by the early Christian writer of the Preaching of Peter:

> [God is] the invisible, who sees all things; uncontained, who contains all things; without needs, of whom all are in need and because of whom they exist; incomprehensible, eternal, imperishable; unmade, who made all by the word of his power.

GOD THE EXTRAVAGANT LOVER

A third central category concerning God emphasizes the generosity of God's love for humankind. It occurs in 28 percent of the texts that centrally concern God, all Presbyterian with one exception. In this category, God freely gives of his love without expectation that it will be earned; indeed, these sermons tell us, God's love cannot be earned. Although this speech has similarities with the two categories discussed above, it contrasts with them in one important respect: It retains hints of the transcendent unknowability of God.

In this set of sermons, God is thoroughly democratic. He loves all regardless of merit and in the same way—freely and equally. No ascribed or achieved qualities of human beings can earn them special attention or support. As one speaker puts it:

> That is the gospel: God has come to find us. He requires no tests to pass—who could pass—and he has wiped clean the slate of the past. He holds nothing against any of us. [SB]

But the nature of God's love is such that it is not merely dispensed equally. An essential element in this category is the characterization of God as an extravagant lover of humankind. The term is used in the sense of its root Latin meaning: To be extravagant is to wander outside, overstep limits, exceed boundaries. As the sermons make clear, the limits against which God's love is measured are the normative limits of *human* behavior. As the sermons mark the contrast between the way in which human beings act toward one another and the behavior of God toward human beings, an essential difference is drawn between the nature of God and the nature of human beings as they live in the world.

Unlike men and women, God is portrayed as devoid of the impulse to weigh or calculate the degree of his love. In the following two excerpts, the figure of the father of the prodigal son is used as a type or metaphor for God:

> When the father sees the son down the road, he drops what he is doing and begins the sprint down the driveway. At that time the jogging craze hadn't hit and it was considered bad form, undignified, for an older man to run. But here he is, running in joyful abandon toward his son. His love is unconditional and uncalculating. [SB]

Further, God is simply motivated by the force of love. No other factors enter into his motivation or behavior—neither knowledge nor other cognitive considerations, neither human ethics nor moral codes. A speaker says:

> [The father] doesn't think about what the neighbors will think or how it will settle with his eldest son. He doesn't worry about morality or psychology or systems approaches to family therapy. He runs! [P]

The contrast between human and divine behavior in the drive to calculate interpersonal responses is sharply drawn in a story told by a Southern Baptist preacher. The story concerns a heterodox version of the Parable of the Prodigal Son (attributed to an "eastern religion") in which:

> When the father sees the son coming home, he doesn't run with abandon to welcome him. Instead, he hides behind a tree. He looks at the son, inspects his appearance, he checks if his hair is cut and face shaven. Then concluding that the son is truly repentant in appearance and spirit, the father comes out from behind the tree and greets his son. [SB]

The message of the heterodox parable, this pastor says, is the same as the norms of behavior that are taught concerning conduct in the secular world: Give each his due. But God operates according to a different set of standards:

[The heretical version of the parable turns] the good news of Jesus into the weary, bad news that we hear every day from every corner—God will love you *if* you are good (Or in a more secular form, you can love yourself *if* you improve yourself). But God is not waiting behind a tree, waiting for us to be good enough before he welcomes us. He is running to embrace us. [SB]

Another pastor uses the figure of the older brother to describe the judgmental human response to wrongdoing and to contrast it with God's response:

Almost as a footnote, the elder brother entered the story. He was incensed at his father's forgiving spirit. He complained loudly that he had been faithful in remaining at home and doing his duty and his father had never expressed any special appreciation for him. Now this is a feeling which you and I have shared. We have seen people who have been irresponsible; who have shirked their duty; who have been a burden on other members of the family or even upon society; who have escaped their "just deserts." If it were left up to us and to the elder brother, there would be absolute justice in the world, and all the prodigals would get what they deserved. [P]

For some speakers whose sermons depict God in this way, the real news, the important point of emphasis, is the radical difference between God's behavior and that of human beings. That God is patently a-rational; that he doesn't evaluate or balance the ledger sheets of human behavior; that he acts according to the rule of love, rather than the human norm of exchange or "just deserts"; all this marks him as different, apart, removed—in other words, as the Other. Not only can human beings never fully emulate his behavior, they cannot even begin to understand it. God's behavior is surprising, shocking, inexplicable within human categories.

As he details this theme of God's unfathomable nature, one preacher echoes the credo of Tertullian, the theologian of the early church, who, in celebrating the paradox of the Christian man-God, claimed that he knew such a God to be true precisely because it was impossible:

[The father] forgiv[es] even before the son can pitch his deal, forgiv[es] before any promises can be pledged, forgiv[es] before any worthiness is proven. Humanly speaking, this is absurd. There ought to be punishment first. The son should apologize, grovel, cry and beg, be vulnerable, and somehow prove that he is really sorry for everything he did. But there is none of that in the story. . . . Jesus was excluding all that, exposing it as utterly irrelevant. [P]

Another speaker continues along these lines:

If you are listening closely to [the parable]—if you really hear what it has to say—you will most likely find it touching. But you will dismiss it as fantasy. Like Walt Disney movies, it doesn't jibe with the world in which we must make our way from day to day. . . . It is the same kind of damp eyed reaction we have to the story of Dumbo or Pinocchio. We'll all go home from church feeling good, but of course no one would consider [applying the message of the story] to their lives in this pay-as-you-go world.

But wait. . . . Jesus was telling a story about God! . . . No wonder God gets relegated to the incredible. No wonder those who profess faith in God are considered naive in the world's terms. No wonder the Apostle Paul would write that the wisdom of God is foolishness with human beings, and vice versa. [P]

Again, as in the prior excerpt, God is humanly "incredible." To this extent, he is also unavailable, inaccessible, inconceivable, and unapprehensible—privative adjectives that force us back to the *via negationis*, the language that can describe only what God is not. But, although the sermon employs this language, it acknowledges its strangeness. Even before the utterance asserts God's humanly absurd nature, the speaker concedes the difficulty contemporary listeners have in accepting this notion. God's incomprehensible actions, his supernatural qualities, belong to the world of myth and fairy tale, to children's fables, to bedtime stories and their modern Technicolor equivalents. So disenchanted has modern life become that only if one suspends one's critical judgment, turns off one's practical cynicism about the "real" world, views things from the magic point of view of a toddler, and relaxes the discipline of one's cognition, can one tune into a story of an elephant that learns to fly, a puppet that becomes a human being, or a God who so loved the world that he died for it. It is a struggle of faith, the speaker suggests, not the guidelines of practical rationality that will get you there. But no matter how out of synch with the assumptions of modern culture, one should believe it because it is so. Its absurdity is an operative part of its truth.

Yet even in this imagery—powerful in its actual form, arguably even more powerful in its potential—God is primarily of instrumental value to human beings. That God is radically different from people is to be celebrated not on its own terms, nor in the abstract, but because the difference benefits humankind. Again, similar to the messages we have seen regarding God as daddy, the benefits are overwhelmingly "this-worldly" and practical. They do not concentrate on God's supernatural role, but are largely limited to comforting hurts and the remission of negative feelings such as anxiety. A Presbyterian pastor says:

> We all know what it means . . . to be in the Far Country of feeling unloved, unwanted, and that particular loneliness of spending the currency of one's life in an effort to feel worthy. . . . The good news is that our worth as persons is a product, not of the work we do, the accomplishments we achieve, or the amount of money we earn . . . [but] of God's love for us. [P]

Another pastor elaborates on the sense of relief one gains from recognition of God's extravagant love. It is the feeling one gets when an onerous burden or obligation has been lifted, a sense of freedom:

> The Gospel of Jesus Christ is a message different from any you and I are likely to hear this week. It is that the God who made us and gave us life and put us here, wants us to know that we are loved, wants us to live in the glorious freedom of children who have no reason to doubt their mother's love, wants us to be so overwhelmed by that love that we live out our lives in laughter and tears of happiness over the surprising wonder of it. [P]

Thus, even though the speech in this category describes the "infinite qualitative difference" between God and humankind, elaborating on God's mercy, his a-rational norm of extravagant love, the difference is tamed in much of this talk as it is made utilitarian and practical for human beings. Even as the human incomprehensibility of God's extravagant love is articulated, it is domesticated into human categories of usefulness. Is there any niche at all in the sermons for portraits that emphasize the transcendent majesty of God? If so, we should expect to find them in the last set to be discussed, those that describe God in his capacity as judge.

GOD THE JUDGE

In a small minority of sermons (16 percent of those that centrally concern God), all Southern Baptist, God is pictured not only as the benevolent father of humankind, but also as a judge who passes sentence on one's future state: elevation to heaven or casting down into hell. Thus, the sermons provide motivation to obey God that exceeds the benefits of psychological comforts in daily life or relief of guilt over hurting his feelings.

Yet although each of the few sermons in this category mentions the possible negative consequences of God's judgment—particularly for the unsaved but also, in much smaller degree, for those Christians who disobey him—God's judgmental functions are not the point of emphasis even here. Most of the sermons in this group draw more dominantly on images of God as daddy or as sufferer, and tend to underplay aspects of God's judgmental characteristics even as they discuss them. Talk about God as judge gives more emphasis to his role in happily granting the reward of heaven to those who accept salvation than to his function in casting the damned into hell.

Even more, when the sermons discuss God's judgment concerning the eternal disposition of the sinner, God's agency in this event tends to be obscured. The connection between God's function as judge and a sinner's punishment in hell is made only by implication. The language here suggests that God's judgment is responsible for the reward of heaven, but human beings alone decide on their course to hell.

As might be expected, much of the speech is addressed to the unsaved, as motives for conversion are given and paths to conversion are detailed. In the excerpt to follow, a pastor addresses the unsaved in an altar call but only indirectly links notions of damnation to God's role as judge:

> This is God's message. He said, "Rejoice, for a soul that was headed for the fires of hell has been rescued and born into the kingdom of God." Now there may be some today who are still lost in your sins; you're still lost and headed for eternal damnation. But today, you'd like to be rescued: forgiven of your sins and given eternal life. [SB]

Another pastor raises the theme of God's negative judgment of the unconverted, but elaborates on it through an Old Testament script that contains only the most general vocabulary:

> Ecclesiastes 11:9 says: "Rejoice, o young man, in thy youth; and let thy heart cheer thee in the days of thy youth, and walk in the ways of thine heart, and in the sight of thine eyes: But know thou, that for all these things God will bring thee into judgment." [SB]

Similarly, the following utterances appeal to the unconverted in a formulation that mixes a strong negative evaluation of sin with an only implicit statement of the result of God's punishment:

> The wages of sin is still death. And God hasn't changed at all his attitude toward sin. You may change your attitude about sin, but God still cries out with a voice of judgment against our sin.[16] [SB]

The relatively weak notion of God's fearsome capabilities regarding judgment is underscored by an almost complete lack of discursive construction of anxiety around one's future state. As we have already seen, the sermons dramatize feelings of anxiety for listeners over many other (this-worldly) aspects of their removal from God, whether they are discussed in the vocabulary of sin or in other formulations. But even when directly referring to the unconverted, only two sermons press on fear of God's judgment by depicting anxiety over salvation, and each text does this only obliquely, as it makes the point indirectly on its way to other issues while buffering the audience from negative feelings.

In the following excerpt, a preacher speaks indirectly about anxiety over the unconverted as he preaches about positive emotions one should have toward the conversion of friends or colleagues. Mainly, he is chastising certain groups in his church for their inadequate reception of new converts:

> I had a young Christian express to me great concern that when a teenager walked the aisle trusting Jesus as savior, the [other] teenagers did not come down to greet him and welcome him into the family of God and their group. No rejoicing? Why not!! [SB]

But while the language of greeting and rejoicing is specific in its reference to particular people, when feelings of anxiety over not being saved are dramatized, the reference is never brought home or personalized for the listener. Instead, it is abstracted through a generalized analogy:

> When astronauts are in space and a problem develops, the world watches and prays and anxiously awaits them . . . when a soul that will remain for eternity has been lost, not in space but in outer darkness and deadly eternal destruction and sin and separation from God; when that lost soul comes to God and is rescued by the power of Jesus for salvation and eternal life, we ought to celebrate. [SB]

Thus, while a model of anxiety is weakly presented, listeners are never fully positioned to participate even in this softened example.

Another example comes from a sermon in the course of explicating the four steps to conversion (the step that is detailed here concerns harnessing the force of the will). Too long to reproduce here in full, the story—set in "Civil War days"—concerns a "wicked slave-master" who is pushed to the brink of nerve-wracking anxiety over salvation by the persistent nagging and vocal prayers of his "old slave, John." As John prays and prays for the slave master's conversion, the master, who previously laughed or shrugged John off, becomes increasingly anxious:

> The old master could not sleep, he awakened in the middle of the night and worried about his soul and his lostedness . . . he was tormented with thoughts. [SB]

The master begs John to tell him how to relieve his fear but then decides he cannot comply with John's instructions:

> He came down and woke John up and said, "I realize that I am a sinner, and I want to be saved. What do I have to do to be saved?"
> And old John replied . . . "All you have to do is to be willing to go down there into the pigpen and get on down into the slop of that old pigpen and get down on your knees and beg God to forgive you."

More sleepless nights finally bring the master to the point of submission:

> And he was sleepless and tormented, and so he came down to John and said, "John, let's go. We're going to the pigpen, because I'll do anything to find peace in my soul."

But John does not exact the price, and thus the story ends:

> John began to jump up and down and said, "Massa [sic], you don't have to go down there. You don't have to do that. All you had to be was *willing* to go there and to do that."

One can, of course, draw various lessons from this rich and revealing story: the ready availability of salvation, as even the most hard-hearted are brought to their knees; the democratic character of witness, as the black slave brings the white master to God; the process of conversion, which demands acts of decision and dignified obedience, not indignities like wallowing around in pigpens; and the essentially private nature of the transformation of conversion, without effects on the structuring of social relationships, as the post-conversion master continues to keep his slaves (at least, there is no evidence to the contrary). More directly germane to my purposes, however, I want to note that, although anxiety over conversion is raised as a topic and indeed is presented for the audience through a detailed description of the slave-master's feelings, the listeners are cushioned and distanced from its force by several devices. First is the temporal remove created by setting the story during the "Civil War"; the characters portrayed here are not contemporary people whose motives and responses will automatically be deemed relevant. Second is the positioning of a slave-master as the anxious would-be convert; it is difficult to imagine an easy identification with a slave-master, even in the privacy of one's own heart. Finally, the story ends without applying the notion of anxiety to the audience; the relevance of the model it presents remains discursively removed. Although undoubtedly displaying various lessons to be taken to heart by the audience, such as the possibilities I have discussed, the story remains positioned largely as a narrative interlude in a long sermon, instead of being an exemplar of anxious feelings over God's judgment.

I turn now to a discussion of God's judgmental qualities that are addressed specifically to believers, that is, to those who are already Christian. Once again, although the message is clearly given that one of God's major functions is to evaluate the actions of men and women and hold them accountable for their deeds, there is little notion of threat. For most speakers, salvation is assured; thus, God's judgmental role is only obliquely relevant. Yet we do find a few ambiguous passages which appear to be addressed to believers, containing the possibility of judgment even for the saved. The following passage includes the strongest formulation in all the sermons of potential negative consequences of God's judgment:

> Man tries to ridicule Hell out of being. "No such thing," he declares. And yet we know that a righteous God must judge the world. . . . There is a heaven, and there is a hell. There is more to life than can be found on this soil. Here we prepare. Here we form the character that will live for eternity. We shall stand before God. We shall be judged. We shall give an account of what we have done on this planet. We will have to answer to God for the talents and time He has entrusted to us. [SB]

Another brief passage—again, a comment in passing—includes the notion that salvation is revocable; hence, God's judgment is ongoingly relevant even to the believer:

To the prodigal, you need to remember that God is not going to forgive you forever, indefinitely, over and over and over again. [SB]

But these formulations are as rare as are elaborations of God's negative judgment on unbelievers. Instead, penalties for straying from the fold are much more likely to be dramatically delineated with respect to consequences in this life, a topic to which I shall return in the next chapter.

CONCLUSIONS

The transcendent, majestic, awesome God of Luther and Calvin—whose image informed early Protestant visions of the relationship between human beings and the divine—has undergone a softening of demeanor throughout the American experience of Protestantism, with only minor interruptions. The speech of the sermons examined in this book gives concrete evidence of the ways in which God's qualities have been mellowed in the contemporary context. Despite variations in emphasis and nuance, strong similarities mark much of this speech. The scope of discussion is almost entirely reduced to God's functions for the private concerns of human beings, relevant to the everyday, practical, commonsense world. These highlight God's primary functions in providing psychological benefits for individual human beings. In two categories of the speech, the one depicting God as a nurturing and supportive daddy and the other explaining God's behavior solely in terms of his extravagant love, God becomes an instrument for the alleviation of the psychological burdens of men and women. He relieves the pain of guilt and self-doubt; he provides membership in a stable "family"; he removes indecision about choices to be made. The strain of practical rationality, of instrumentalism, is apparent in this speech.

A third strand of imagery portrays God in terms of his inner states. Here the sermons emphasize the accessibility of human beings to the thoughts and feelings of the divine, even, in some cases, urging human empathy with God. These portrayals of God's subjectivity, and the nature of God's subjectivity as consonant with human experiences, are functional for adapting religious speech to contemporary sensibilities.

These depictions work to foreclose notions that God is removed from human beings. In asserting essential similarities between the very subjectivities of God and human beings, they serve to remove any residual notions of mystery or awe that have traditionally accompanied transcendent portrayals of God. This imagery renders a God whose characteristics still belong within the category of "religious"—that is, he is not "explained away" through relativizing scientific or social scientific discourse—yet who is relatively demythologized, available to human beings' simple comprehension based on their intuitive understanding of their own subjectivity.

But there is also evidence of resistance to these tendencies in some sermons. Some Presbyterian preachers refuse to reduce God fully to human categories. God's behavior, they say, cannot be fully understood by human beings, since it conforms to no known human principle. These sermons teach that while human beings can categorize God's behavior according to a single element, the rule of love, they can never fully comprehend his "reasons," since God's love, in its overwhelming benevolence, is simply "shocking." An important element of God's mystery—his transcendence and his supernatural nature—is thereby preserved.

Another form of partial resistance lodges in a few Southern Baptist sermons, which retain the awesomeness and judgmental qualities of the demanding, transcendent God. Here, although God forgives penitents for their lapses, he is presented as the one before whom men and women stand in judgment, and to whom individuals answer for the conduct of their lives. Although the sermons do not emphasize this theme, there is the suggestion that this God demands obedience, and is capable not only of love, but also punishment.

Images of Christian Faith
in the Contemporary World

IN *The Heretical Imperative*, the sociologist of religion Peter Berger tells a story about a contemporary Indonesian villager. Not long ago, had the villager wished to go visiting, he would have hopped into his bull cart to seek out relatives in a nearby settlement. Nowadays, however, the villager with wanderlust and enough money can board a jet to Malaysia or the Philippines or indeed, via connecting flights, to virtually any country in the world.[1]

The metaphor of the Third World air traveler, Berger writes, neatly symbolizes in certain ways the impact of modern times on people's lives. Contemporary life brings with it the constant demand of making choices, as a result of its multiple offerings: choices about one's travel destinations, leisure activities, occupation, the configuration of one's family—choices about virtually every aspect of conduct throughout life.

To live in our world is to live in a world of pluralism. No longer do a small number of relatively stable institutions mark out the contours of appropriate belief and practice for the majority of people. Instead, the social world has splintered into segments and subcultures in which people adhere to different beliefs, traditions, and definitions of appropriate behavior. As people come into contact with an array of cultures—as they inevitably do in a modern society, through personal contact with others or through the mass media—their own traditions tend to lose the element of taken-for-grantedness that once sustained them. In the absence of strong social support for one's traditions, for one's view of the world, these beliefs begin to lose plausibility.

In the world of pluralism, even such fundamental beliefs as religious faith can be thrown into confusion. One's neighbors and work colleagues are as likely to adhere to a different religious tradition as to one's own, or perhaps to none at all. Even if a person lives in a relatively homogeneous community or confines social contacts to people of the same creed, the daily newspaper and the programs shown on television provide vicarious contact with persons of different backgrounds. Thus, for many, even religious self-identification is no longer taken for granted. Multiple, sometimes contradictory, modes of thought and behavior offer themselves up as alternatives. For many contemporary people, making choices about daily events, about the course of life, even about the great existential questions of self-definition, faith, and reality, is the normal state of affairs.

Thus, the array of options for belief and behavior available in our world pose dilemmas for speakers attempting to promote particular formulations for religious adherence. For counterposed to the putatively timeless, objective, and universal tenets and behavioral prescriptions of the Christian faith are the attractions of the personalized and relativized ideologies of secular life. Within a culture that values individual choice-making based on personal preference, how can pastors present an ostensibly objective and collectively valid Christian message? How can they communicate the place of the Christian faith within a changing, option-laden, world?

Responding to the World

The challenge posed by secular culture to an appropriate Christian life is exacerbated by conditions of modern times. But of course the challenge is not unique to modernity. In every age, in every culture, Christians have found it necessary to confront the problems society raises for Christian belief. In his classic study, *Christ and Culture*, H. Richard Niebuhr examines the variety of approaches that Christian theologians and practitioners have adopted to these problems over the centuries. The approaches range from rejection of the world (as in monasticism) to a thoroughgoing accommodation of Christian messages to secular norms (as in some quarters of modern liberal Protestantism) to positions in between in which it is acknowledged that proper Christian faith and the world are simultaneously at odds with, and reconcilable to, each other—positions that are rooted in Augustine, Luther, and Calvin. In these middle formulations, the relationship between Christian faith and the secular world involves a dynamic process of interaction, struggle, and synthesis, as Christian belief informs, transmutes, or operates in creative tension with, the norms of secular culture.

The sermons examined in this book run the gamut in their depictions of Christian responses to the world of secular twentieth-century America, as pastors tailor to contemporary situations the general strategies

Niebuhr discusses. The approaches in the sermons extend from those that illustrate the effortless melding of Christ and culture to those that vehemently deny the suitability even of contact between one and the other.

In one group of sermons, including nearly all of those by Presbyterians, the contemporary world presents few obstacles to an appropriate realization of Christian faith. In this speech, the problem is not one of tension between faith and culture, but of properly utilizing faith to get the most one can from the natural and social world.

In a second group of sermons, the multiplicity of paths offered within the world is a potential source of troubles: specifically, of a psychological sense of homelessness and alienation that results from attempting to gain satisfaction through the world. At work in this speech is a partial reframing of the nature of religion, as speakers suggest that only Christian belief can provide overarching significance for human existence. While people are competent to act within the world, its offerings are unable to give lasting and satisfying meaning to people's lives.

For a third group, the world is to be regarded warily, since it is a potential snare, a source of loneliness and separation if the wrong path is selected. The core metaphor in this category, prevalent among Southern Baptists, is that of lostness: physical separation from the protective community and even more, from the protective "walk" with God, and psychological torment that results from the anxiety of being alone in a vast and confusing world. Although this is not a discourse of total separation from the world, it does teach that one must be ever vigilant to remain within the enclaves of safety.

A fourth group voices complete opposition to the world and urges withdrawal from it. In this speech, the world is a place of moral ugliness and decay, defiling those who enter it. Only by shunning the world can one hope to live a properly Christian life and attempt to be holy; while those who truck with the world are, as it were, citizens of Sodom.

Before turning to the details of these categories, I should point out an important similarity that connects them. As in speech about God, the focus of this discourse, too, is the individual, as he chooses lifestyles, paths, or correct or incorrect ways of acting. This emphasis on the individuated actor constricts the dimensions of the relevant world. Only in a tiny minority of sermons is the world a place of social concerns and interactions, in which choices made about behavior have to do with social issues such as justice or equality.[2] Likewise, it is rare for the sermons to talk explicitly about the world in terms of divergent, contradictory, or competing *traditions*, in which the agents are collectivities rather than individuals. Notions of tradition or community are implicit in some of this speech (as, in the fourth category, Southern Baptists speak about the protective circle of their world), but rarely do they arise as a matter of direct attention.

Instead, in the great majority of sermons, the world is portrayed solely from the perspective of the individual person: the competing frameworks of belief and behavior which are offered to her, and from which she needs to select. Instead of making arguments based on tradition, pastors appeal to their listeners on grounds of benefits or risks to the individual. To that extent, at least, almost all the sermons accept the positioning of religion as a matter of "consumer choice."

Thirty-three of the forty-seven sermons contain imagery on the topic of the world: 69 percent of the Presbyterian sermons and 71 percent of the Southern Baptist sermons.[3]

The World as Unproblematic

The category of the world as unproblematic occurs in 83 percent of the Presbyterian sermons that offer imagery about the world, and in only one Southern Baptist sermon (5 percent). In this set of sermons, there is no particular tension between Christian faith and worldly culture or social arrangements. This assertion is not so much made as implied, in most of the sermons; speakers do not endorse the cultural and social status quo so much as they produce speech about Christian life in the world that renders it unremarkable. In their speech, the world is naturalized. It is neither evil nor good, neither hurtful nor beneficial with respect to encouraging a properly Christian life; it simply is. In all its aspects—social, cultural, and physical alike—the world is the taken-for-granted backdrop against which one lives a Christian life, described here almost exclusively in terms of one's inner self and daily relationships with family, work colleagues, and a small circle of neighbors and friends. The sermons provide numerous narratives and commentary about people in the routine events of life—shopping for pets, eating dinner at the family table, gathering at reunions, praying privately or with others, working the 9:00 to 5:00, fishing for brook trout, playing football, camping out, dining in restaurants—in which the behavior of Christians coexists comfortably and seamlessly with the norms of ordinary secular behavior. (These are, of course, scenes of middle-class America, with the leisure and money for hobbies, dining out, giving children allowances for making purchases, and taking vacations.)

But how might one square acceptance of the world with the demands of Christian living? The response of these sermons is to suggest that living a proper Christian life is more a matter of adopting an attitude of modest enjoyment of the world's offerings than of making behavioral sacrifices. Just about absent here is the topic of renunciation or change in conduct that a worldly person must make to conform his secular behavior to the norms of Christian life. There are only a few mentions of such necessary modifications in the entire group of Presbyterian sermons. Almost without exception, the modifications involve minor adjustments in daily routine, instead of altering or challenging normative behavior in the world.

The problem these speakers raise with their listeners is that of establishing the correct balance of worldly and spiritual activities, not that of any of the activities in themselves. For example, in the excerpt that follows, a pastor offers a communal prayer in which he models for his congregants the need to make time for God. Note that none of the worldly activities mentioned in his catalogue—the ordinary conduct of middle-class life—is even remotely criticized:

> O Lord our God, how much we need you. Why is it we get so hung up making a living, trying to get things done around the house, being sociable, getting an education, and making ends meet, that we scarcely make any time to be with you? [P]

Similarly, another pastor implicitly urges his listeners to sort out their priorities and leave more time in busy schedules for experiencing positive Christian emotions. Here, the demands of Christianity that impinge on life in the world are not only few and only sketchily mentioned, they are also overwhelmingly pleasant:

> I fear that many of us are . . . losing ourselves in our work. Putting jobs always ahead of joy, work ahead of love. [P]

Note once again that jobs and work in the secular world are never questioned or criticized. The problem is that these tasks have become unbalanced in the calculus of living, so that their emphasis provides little time for—for what, exactly? Not for any spiritual activities that might provide tension between worldly and spiritual affairs, such as obedience to God or making sacrifices on behalf of one's faith, but for taking full advantage of the personal benefits of Christian living, such as feelings of joy and love.[4]

On this point, we should note any mention in this speech of constraints on worldly behavior that Christians must impose on themselves. Explicit talk about such limits appears only infrequently; the Christian is rarely asked to refrain from secular activities. The most pronounced example appears in the following excerpt, as Christian joy is contrasted with another set of feelings—the escapist pleasures of the world. This is one of the few examples in the Presbyterian sermons that construct a boundary between Christian life and worldly life; but notice exactly what it is about secular life that the Christian is expected to shun. In this speech, the few disapproved behaviors are caricatured; these discursive constructions act to weaken the relevance of the formulation to listeners (not to mention the surprising effect of the first three sentences):

How fantastic to know that God wants us to laugh, to be cheerful. Sometimes when I am with friends I become hilarious and giggle uncontrollably. I get so tickled I embarrass myself and usually those around me. . . . I believe celebration among Christian families and church families can be resurrected! Let me emphasize that celebration in Scripture refers to something far deeper than our society's cheap, drunken, drug-taking, obscene sources of enjoyment—it is being secure in God's unconditional love! Christian merriment is permanent—it doesn't end when the narcotic wears off. [P]

In addition to noting the abbreviated and unelaborated list of constraints given here—which might be summarized as "don't drink to excess, don't do drugs, and don't be sexually promiscuous"—we should turn our attention to the reason implied behind these suggested limits. They introduce another important theme in these sermons: The purpose of Christian faith is not to contradict the world, but, rather, to lead one to a heightened enjoyment of it. Why should one shun drink, drugs, and sexual promiscuity? It is not because these behaviors violate one's relationship with God, or are contrary to God's word, or defile the holiness or purity of the person: It is because they are inadequate to the purpose of providing joy ("Christian merriment is permanent—it doesn't end when the narcotic wears off"). In this utterance, the goal of human behavior in the world is marked as a type of hedonism—the experience of pleasure, merriment, and hilarity. And the problem implied with drugs, alcohol, and sexual experiences is that their gratification is too shallow and too brief. The excerpt appears to suggest that one should not settle for pharmaceutical or sexual means of pleasure when one can in fact seek out the all-encompassing, thorough, and long-lasting outcomes, through appropriate Christian faith and practice, of what is in effect a "natural high" ("How fantastic that God wants us to laugh, to be cheerful. Sometimes . . . I become hilarious and giggle uncontrollably.").

To be fair to this pastor's speech, I should note that the pleasures accruing from Christian faith, while they do not require practitioners to abandon much worldly behavior, nevertheless are rooted in an ongoing and transforming relationship with God. The "natural high" offered to the listener stems from conduct which, in some respects, transcends mundane experience. It is one's "decision to aggressively trust God" (as the preacher puts it elsewhere in his sermon) that allows the experience of pleasure to flow. One stays on the crest of the "natural high" by the moment-by-moment experience of God's love, by the continuous realization of being part of God's "Forever Family," by the constant reminder that one is forgiven of wrongdoings. As the pastor puts it, drawing on Scripture as the authority for the joyous aspect of Christian living:

> Joy becomes the dominant theme of our life on earth. Surprise, merriment, joy, laughter are part of what it means to be in relationship with God. Scripture calls us to rejoice, to laugh, to exhibit cheerfulness and joy. Personally I love to laugh! I am thrilled when I hear the commandment, 'You shall rejoice before the Lord . . . rejoice always . . . be glad and rejoice forever.' (ellipses in original) [P]

There is a note of supernaturalism here, of transcendence of the purely mundane. Yet the "natural high" achieved through God accomplishes the purpose of allowing one to go about one's business in the world with unrelenting cheerfulness. As the speaker delivers this utterance, and as those persuaded of its validity wear their faces of joy in daily life, the advertisement of the "natural high" that stems from God extends a powerful membership appeal: The Christian life is not one of sacrifice and self-denial concerning the things of the world; the Christian life is positively fun! As a Christian colleague of mine put it in interpreting this passage, "One can be a good Christian and still have a good time."

Less obviously, and in more muted tones, the imagery of the "natural high" undergirds much additional talk in this group of sermons about the Christian life. Where the templates of Christianity are held up for fit against the backdrop of the world—something that seldom happens—the norms of Christian living are explored as possibilities for heightening, without actually transcending, one's positive experience of life in the world. Chief among the qualities of Christian life, some sermons suggest, is that it teaches one how to experience spontaneous enjoyment. It gives one an appreciation for nature, for the company of other people, and for the little daily pleasures of life. At the heart of a sermon preached by a Presbyterian pastor is the message that contemporary people, like the father in the parable, should "celebrate what is found." In the following excerpt, appropriate Christian life in the world is characterized by enjoyment of the moment and a will to seek out opportunities in the future. We should note the vocabulary of humanistic psychology suggested by images of "growth and development" and of achieving satisfying interpersonal relationships. We should also mark the conflation of potentially spiritual concerns with secular humanistic talk about the Christian life as self-education:

> Words like these [referring to expressions of regret such as, "If only I had worked harder in school"] show that we root our identity, that we live our lives in the past, lives of sentimentality and reminiscence. Words like these ignore the true emotion of life in the present, the challenge of new opportunity, the work of forgiveness and reconciliation, the risks of new relationships or of renewing old ones. They suggest that we lack the courage to learn. The Christian life is one of continual seeking, a continual education process.[5] [P]

This sermon goes on to give examples of the proper Christian attitude toward the world. Using the theme of the prodigal son who is found again to teach a lesson about how to live one's daily life, it provides instruction on enjoying and celebrating worldly experiences. In the following excerpt, the Christian message is tantamount to a set of principles that one lays over the experiences of the natural world in order to get more out of them—which, in effect, means properly enjoying them:

> Celebrate what is found. Rejoice in the loves of your life: your children, your spouse; your parents; your friends. It's hard to imagine, isn't it, true lovers who do not laugh. Rejoice in the gifts of each day: good health, a place to live and work; food to eat; a good book; a chance encounter; the beauty of creation. [P]

Note, again, that the list of events and experiences to be enjoyed by the Christian in the world is utterly naturalized, as interpersonal experiences, the health of the body, and aesthetic, intellectual, and physical pleasures.

The theme of the "natural high" is further developed in the next excerpt; however, it contains a bit more transformative imagery than the others we have seen. The things of the world are elevated to a transcendent level by being infused with divine purpose ("to point toward God in all we do"). Once again, though, there is no hint in the message of contradiction between Christianity and the ordinary affairs of life, no notion of the demands of Christian practice. The emphasis is not on the glorification of God, but on people's enjoyment of life in the world. Note that the speaker even tells listeners that Christianity ought to provide ongoing pleasure, prodding them to say that it "feels good" to be Christian:

> Our purpose for living is to point toward God in all we do—and enjoy doing it—enjoy him. To feel good about the life He's given us to live. . . . Have you enjoyed being a Christian this week? Can you remember a time this week when you thought, "Boy, I'm glad I'm a Christian. Boy, it feels good!"? [P]

In line with the representation of the world as unproblematic for the practice of Christian life are depictions in these sermons of the world's benignity. The pastors' main opportunity for portraying the world occurs in the context of discussing the journey of the prodigal son into the far country, where, the parable tells us, the lad encounters famine and deprivation, and is eventually forced into a job tending swine. The biblical text virtually demands that pastors describe the world's potential malevolence, as one speaker notes:

> The picture in the minds of Jesus' audience was all too vivid. In a real famine, the kind they knew something about, shoe leather, rotten meat, and plain garbage are all eaten. Straying animals are slaughtered and devoured raw. Children are sold into slavery to keep them from starving to death. The corpses fill the streets. . . . That is famine! [P]

But the sermons of the Presbyterian pastors rarely develop this theme. Their discussions of the prodigal son's experiences disregard ideas of cruelty or suffering, and instead, describe the boy merely as having a hard time or undergoing an unpleasant experience. For example, one pastor mitigates the boy's sufferings, hence the potential cruelty of the world, by viewing the story in terms of the difficulty a modern youngster might have finding employment:

When the famine came [the prodigal son] joined the unemployment lines and searched desperately for a job. Finally he got a job taking care of pigs. . . . That was the lowest job there was. But a job was better than no job, so the young spendthrift took it. [P]

Other pastors race without elaboration through the plot of the story, with little to say about the remarkable situation in which the young man finds himself. In the following excerpt, for example, note how the son's plight is minimized through the vocabulary of understatement:

[When in the far country], the prodigal son took up with a wild crowd and quickly ran through his fortune in reckless and extravagant spending. Eventually he found himself lonely, hungry [and] ashamed. [P]

In the next excerpt, the suffering the world inflicts on the prodigal son is emphasized less than the lack of dignity he experiences as he feeds the pigs:[6]

[The prodigal son] travels off to a far country . . . and there he falls in with the wrong crowd. At first it seemed like the good life, but then his funds started to dwindle, and before he could even think about getting a job to get him over the rough spots, a famine hits, and everybody seems to be out of work. The best he can do as far as employment is concerned is to work in the stock yards as a pig feeder. There's not much dignity in that line of work, especially for a boy brought up in the Hebrew tradition and the belief that swine were ritually unclean. [P]

Indeed, far from being malevolent, the natural world is sometimes depicted in these sermons as a vehicle for people's contemplation, a means through which human beings can learn who they really are. In the next excerpt, a pastor uses nature to teach listeners how to "get back to their feelings"; nature allows human beings to become more fully in touch with their inner selves, since it is a benign force through which people can plumb their inner depths to gain self-awareness:

All of us are, to a great extent, out of touch with our senses. Gestalt therapy is saying things like this: "Sit still for a moment. Listen to what's happening around you right now. Look at the faces of the people, what they are feeling, what they are saying. Did you hear the sound of that bird a moment ago? Did you hear the sound of the cricket, or the rustle of the leaves in the late afternoon breeze. . . . Are you in touch with your own feelings? Are you angry inside? Do you feel joy about life, or sadness? [P]

This passage leads to a point I want to make in summary about the preceding portraits of Christian life in the world. I mentioned earlier the middle-class orientation of the language of the sermons. Here, I would add that this language couches certain assumptions about the standing of human beings in the natural world. These sermons radiate an unproblematic optimism about Christian faith in the world not only because their portrait of that faith is so accommodated to worldly norms; the optimism also stems from the assumption that human beings have mastery over their social, cultural, and even natural environments. The choice-making demanded by the world of social order and culture, and the potential threats present in nature, pose no difficulties for Christian life, in this speech, because of an implicit understanding that the demands and threats of the world have been tamed by the very persons who are the recipients of the sermons' messages. The talk suggests that human beings "like us" are competent to deal with the pluralism and complexity of the world; they know how to navigate a path among the thickets of multiple offerings, they know how to allow faith to coexist with concerns of mundane life. There are no dangers in interacting with the world.

Thus, because issues of control over the world are not a problem in this speech—since control is instead assumed—the difficulties remaining for Christians are largely those of balance: how to counterweigh one's rational control over the world, as evidenced by the daily concerns of job and family, with the ability to "go with the flow," enjoy life, experience emotional release, take the time to "smell the roses." As the sermons see it, this is one of the important functions of religious experience for human beings: to enable the release of genteel affect into the rational control of one's daily experience of the world. It is a way of temporarily and "spontaneously" allowing emotion back into a controlled (and controlling) life, a way of letting go. How different this point of view is from those expressed in other sermons we shall explore in the subsequent sections of this chapter.

The Frustration of Meaning in the World

Unlike the first set of sermons, the next group draws an explicit boundary between the mundane world and the realm of spiritual truths. Indeed, all the rest of the sermons in the sample mark some sort of symbolic segregation between the two worlds: the natural world of human beings and the spiritual world of God and the godly. Not only do the features of the human world and the God-world differ from each other, they are also, in various ways, incompatible. Thus, in presenting a dark vision of the effects of the world on the possibilities for Christian faith, all the remaining sermons describe life in the human world as a problem for proper Christians.

The small set of sermons examined in this section display particularly creative solutions to the tensions of contemporary mainline Protestant speech. (Twenty percent of the Southern Baptist sermons and six percent of the Presbyterian sermons are represented in this group.) While the speakers strive to maintain a relatively unaccommodated version of Christian faith, they also wish to make that theology relevant to concerns of contemporary people—to discuss the effects of modern life on the individual's psyche. Their solution is in part to recast the role of religion in modern life, along lines noted in my discussion of reframing in chapter two. In the pastors' speech about the contrasting spheres of human world and God-world, religion is constituted not primarily as a system of objective truths (although this idea is not completely absent), but, instead, as the means by which people can find significance in their lives. Christian faith, in this speech, delivers people not so much from sin or evil or spiritual error as from the meaninglessness that is held to characterize the secular world of choices.

This talk erects symbolic boundaries between the two spheres by marking a division between two sets of psychological states of the men and women who inhabit them. The sermons premise that all people look for meaning in their lives. But the potential for finding meaning lies only within the realm of spiritual truth. A person who depends on worldly affairs to provide an emotionally and intellectually satisfying account of his life is in for a grave disappointment; the natural world is incapable of supplying a framework within which to find ultimate significance. Dependence on the world of secular culture leads to feelings of disorder, alienation, confusion, and most important, the hopelessness and anomie of meaninglessness. Neither the goods of the world nor the day-to-day activities of ordinary life, nor even knowledge of the inner self—except as the self is constituted as a mirror of God—can help people make sense of their condition and the events of their lives.

Misguided Quests

As he examines the motives for the prodigal son's departure from home, one preacher suggests that modern men and women have more

reasons than simple rebellion for their flights from God, and more resources to draw on in their search for alternatives:

> We feel ill-at-ease with our own faces, and we run out and buy some
> new make-up or grow a beard. We feel ill-at-ease with our own bodies,
> and we run out and join an exercise club or buy some Jordache jeans.
> We feel ill-at-ease with our personalities, so we mask our dis-ease in
> alcohol and drugs or we affect a boisterous public personality; but it is
> a masquerade. We feel ill-at-ease even at home, but *Better Homes and
> Gardens* cannot make our homes feel more like home. [SB]

In the scriptural parable, the prodigal son's journey takes the form of
a single circuit. The son leaves home for the far country; abides there
for awhile, depleting his money; bottoms out in the pigpen; "comes to
himself," deciding to return to his father; and journeys, and is wel-
comed, home. But the condition of men and women in the modern
context is far more complicated than that of the young man in Scripture, the pastor suggests through the structure of this excerpt. The vari-
eties and complexities of modern culture spawn myriad versions of the
far country, the alien place to which one goes, seeking (but not realizing) satisfaction. Indeed, people may spend their entire lives migrating
from one foreign locale to another, searching for the elusive sense of
fulfillment, never "coming home."

In the sermon, the modern world offers the itinerant a variety of
initially promising but ultimately disappointing ports of call. The
excerpt touches several bases of the contemporary middle-class rep-
ertoire of the quest for self-knowledge, self-expression, and self-improvement. Here we see the glorification of the body and attempts at
perfecting it, both through artifice ("we buy some new make-up") and
"natural" means ("we join an exercise club"); the expression of personal tastes and the creation of a personal aesthetic, in the design and
decoration of one's home; the culture of consumerism, seeking gratification through the purchase and ownership of goods; and familiar
mechanisms of transcending (or sublimating) feelings of discontent,
such as using drugs or alcohol, or dissembling to others. It is not that
these offerings of the secular world, these possibilities of action, must
simply be infused with a spiritual outlook to make them more likely to
yield meaning, satisfaction, or pleasure, as in the first set of sermons. It
is that secular activity is incapable of providing any of these rewards,
no matter how it is transformed.

The structure of this excerpt highlights another element of the failure
of secular quests: The speech here turns from one alternative to an-

other, with heightened narrative speed. The syntax of this excerpt mirrors the problem of the sheer variety of options that the secular world holds out to men and women in search of meaning. People try out, and reject, alternative sources of satisfaction in a feverish spell of activity in the world, monitoring themselves and changing paths when the selected option does not work. The end result is not meaning, but exhaustion and frustration; the sermon teaches that it is not possible to assemble a meaningful Christian life out of the fragmented offerings of secular culture.

The hopeless task of seeking meaning from the world is underscored, in this sermon, by talk that elaborates on the lack of "t" between the offerings of the world and essential human nature. I shall examine in greater detail the portraits of human nature in the sermons in chapter six. For now, it will suffice to show that this preacher sees an awkward overlay between human needs and the potential satisfactions that the world can supply. For although people may seek meaning through secular activities, deep in their hearts they know that the world is not "home":

> I would interpret much of the dis-ease of our age, the anxiety and estrangement rampant in the modern world, as a sense of displacement, the feeling of being a refugee, strangers inside our own skin, strangers in a strange land. We do not feel quite at home, not with God, nor with ourselves nor in the world. [SB]

Note how this excerpt—though it is rooted in the psychology of the individual through its articulation of feelings of anxiety and alienation—takes the listener beyond individual feeling-states to construct a far more objective problem. Unlike the first set of sermons we have examined, the difficulties constructed in this speech are not about how to "feel good," but how to "feel right." In the former construct, there is no frame of reference outside the immediate affect, the instant knowledge of an individual person's psychological apparatus. But in the notion of "feeling right," or "feeling at home," there is implied the need to be connected, to be centered in a context larger than the individualized needs of the self. According to the sermon, this is precisely the problem that the world creates for the human species. For it cannot supply the essential need—the achievement of the permanence and orientation of citizenship, as opposed to the constant migration, the uncertain status, the alien experiences, of the refugee.

There is another way in which the language of the excerpt communicates a universality of human need, and thus a set of troubles with respect to the world, that surpasses the level of individual drives toward satisfactions. The pun created by the use of the term *dis-ease* suggests an objectification of the problem. At the same time that the hyphenated word conveys a private, internal feeling of discomfort and distress, the unified word suggests an objective difficulty, a difficulty of the body. Not only do people in the world "feel wrong"; something *is* wrong. Because the problems are both objective and total, a crisis is constructed that is insoluble in terms of the world: The world is emptied of the promise of meaning.

Similarly, for another speaker, the quest for meaning and satisfaction in the secular world is not merely bound to disappoint; it makes a victim of the seeker. In this sermon, there is an equal sense of failure, disappointment, and hopelessness concerning activity in the world as in the first sermon examined in this section. But it comprises an even bleaker version of the possibilities of finding meaning in the world. This message teaches that not just secular searches for meaning, but any secularly-anchored *hope* at all, ends in failure. The things of the world are profoundly deceptive; they are temptations clothed in pretty wrapping paper. But temptation, in this excerpt, does not lead so much to error or sin as to the radical loss of hope:

> It is a good time to come back; we've said, "give me what is my due," and life has disappointed us, over and over again. Clovis Chappel once told of a community Christmas party in a small village. Everyone was there, including a mentally handicapped young man who was crudely and cruelly called the village idiot. That night the largest and most impressively wrapped gift had his name on it. He was so excited. Eagerly he peeled away the wrapping and opened the large box. It was empty. They had played a trick on him. They all laughed. Terrible story, yes, but not so terrible as the ones in real life. The world is full of empty boxes and we have taken turns playing the village idiot. Hands reach out . . . empty boxes . . . give me the goods. . . . I must see life. . . . I must find myself. . . . Soon we learn it was not life at all; just pitiful beings staring into empty boxes. (ellipses in original) [SB]

In this excerpt, attempts to find meaning do not end in failure only for the willful men and women who think they can find significance for their lives through their own strenuous efforts. They also cruelly disappoint even the intellectually and morally innocent (symbolized by the village idiot). This raises the theme of life in the world as an arena of the victimization of the innocent, a prominent Southern Baptist idea.

Lost in the World

The theme of being lost in the world appears in 66 percent of the Southern Baptist sermons and six percent of the Presbyterian sermons. In this category, the secular world is presented as a realm of confusion and danger in which, without correct guidance, people become inescapably lost. In this state, human beings become detached from any locus of orientation, from all significant relationships—with other people, to be sure, but particularly with God. Without this grounding, human beings are beset by the world's complexities and troubles. Because people are portrayed in these sermons as incapable of dealing with complexity, they lose the ability to chart the course of their lives with purpose and control, and are marked as prey for the evils of the world.

To be lost means to fall between the cracks of categories of existence, adhering neither to the good and correct, nor to the evil and wrong. The median place between these two categories—the metaphor for the mundane realm of choices—is a space of purgatory, of nothingness, that resonates with danger. The perils of this state of liminality are described as real, objective, and physical in nature. At the same time, they carry with them the psychological correlates of unbearable feelings of disconnectedness and terror, described with the powerful poetic evocation that traditionally has been reserved for portraying the torments of hell. To leave the realm of the correct and good and to seek an alternative formulation of life is to make a categorical error; to abandon "areas of form" for "areas of formlessness" is both to open oneself to danger and to violate the order inherent in the natural universe.[7]

In the sermons discussed in this section, confronting danger is the price one pays for departure from one's appropriate place, from a proper conception of the good, and from a proper relationship with God. The risk of danger, and the accompanying experience of terror, are described as natural consequences of searching for alternative definitions of self and conduct. The natural world itself encodes God-given definitions of right behavior, and supplies punishment for those who seek alternatives. Because the penalties of lostness are "hard-coded" in the very nature of things, they are impossible to escape.

Metaphors of Lostness

One preacher describes the process of becoming lost with the aid of two metaphors, those of the department store and the wandering child.

They work together to create a world of complexity and confusion in which people may easily lose their way:

> A child just follows the attractions in the department store. He knows what he's looking for, he's looking for the toy department. He starts in women's lingerie [because he is in the department store with his mother]. Now what he has to do is he looks for something a lot more needful than women's lingerie. . . . So he looks for something that appeals more and he keeps looking and he follows each attraction and he has to go through the shoe department and he wanders through the jewelry department and he gets to the hardware and he pushes the lawnmower around. Finally he gets to the toy department, but he doesn't really know where the toy department is. He's lost. [SB]

The metaphor of the department store masterfully captures the world's size and complexity. From the point of view of a child, the store is vast beyond measure—a maze of levels, corridors, and sections. Its interior architecture appears spatially confused. Display shelves are set up on angles, selling floors are arranged for maximum exposure to merchandise, and escalators are placed so that shoppers must walk the length of the store. Most adult shoppers have had, at one time or another, the disorienting sensation of not knowing exactly where they are. For a child who is alone, the department store can feel like a labyrinth.

In addition, the metaphor of the department store communicates the superficial appeal of the world's overwhelming variety. In this idea are entailed notions of the allure of consumer objects, of glitter, of attractive packaging, of goods placed at eye level, available within easy reach. In short, the metaphor of the department store depicts misguided desire: The person is reduced to the category of potential consumer tempted to wander endlessly, just as the young child looks for "needful" things in one department after another. Customers seek that which they think they want, only to realize that the wrong item has been selected. But because there are more departments to search through, the temptation remains to keep on searching, searching, searching (just as the popular slogan exhorts one to "shop until you drop").

As in one of the sermons examined in the previous section, the depiction of endless, fruitless searching is heightened by the excerpt's narrative ow. The running together of equally weighted clauses, as the child's wanderings are described, suggests mimicry and debunking of the hasty trial and equally swift abandonment of choices in the secular world ("he keeps looking and he follows each attraction and he has to

71

go through the shoe department and he wanders through the jewelry department . . . "). The child roams through one department after another; when he is dissatisfied, still more options are available. The only end to his journey arrives when he becomes hopelessly lost.

The second metaphor in this excerpt, that of the wandering child, is equally strategic. It evokes key human tendencies that make it possible to find oneself in the position of the lost boy in the department store. In this sermon, all men and women are innately like a small child. They are ruled by impulses that make it difficult to check desires. Impelled by the immediacy of their wants and needs, they stray off the path and meander endlessly among disorienting corridors. People are neither evil nor sinful here; they are merely misguided. Lacking the stability of the familiar and the certainty of orientation, they wander into strange places and cannot extricate themselves in order to "come home."

Thus, the two central metaphors construct a sense of lostness as an essential element of life in the world, for those who do not have the correct conception of God. Becoming lost results both from the innate qualities of human beings and the objective nature of worldly things. As we shall see in chapter five, attribution of a double causality to lostness helps soften the blame for sin by shifting some of the responsibility for sin from human agents to the inherent complexity of the world.

In the sermon I have been examining, the story of the lost child is quickly extended into a description of the feeling-states of lostness. The child's experience of terror becomes universalized, so that it is held to characterize everyone's childhood experience:

> Did you ever get lost as a child? You know then what it means to be truly lost. I mean not knowing where you are and it's one of the most terrifying predicaments that you can have happen to you. To wonder if you'll ever find your way back home or ever find anybody you know again is an unforgettable experience. [SB]

In the excerpt that follows, from the same sermon, the feelings of the universal childhood experience are further generalized to characterize the feelings of all human beings in the condition of being lost. For the moment, I will note only the totality of the description, which is in part effected through elaborative detail and repetition:

> Lostedness is a desperate and helpless and horrifying experience. If you've ever been lost, you know it's scary. Being separated from the familiar. Not knowing where you are. Being separated from your

loved ones. Not knowing where they are. Separated from any purpose or meaning in life. That's scary. The lost sheep gradually did it. Without even realizing what was happening. So many times that's the way man does it. Then he wakes up all alone. He may be in a crowd, but he's all alone. Worse than that, unprotected. Out in no man's land, no friends, no one to watch over you, subject to all kinds of horrors and dangers. Horrors. Easy prey. Have you seen stories of the young girls that wander off, leave home, bright lights, dreams of an acting career or a modeling career and they end up on some strip of prostitution. Victims, dreams tossed aside. [SB]

We should note that, here, lostness is formulated in absolute terms. The nature of the world is such that one cannot become partially lost. To take the first step out of the realm of the familiar is eventually to lose everything, and to experience the sense of utter aloneness that follows from segregation from what is known. As soon as one becomes separated from one's familiar surroundings and family, one also loses the sublime elements of purpose and meaning, and even the ultimate anchor, that of God. And to go in the opposite direction in the analysis of this series, the risks of wandering away are not only the loss of existential meaning, but the pragmatic, everyday connections of family and home. (This is, of course, a discursive elaboration of the idea of the "slippery slope.")

Another aspect of the absolute nature of being lost is closely linked to the first. Lostness as an objective experience of separation is connected to internal states of desperation, helplessness, and terror. One cannot escape these strong, frightening emotions, these feelings (reminiscent of early childhood) of powerlessness and loss of control. In this talk, there is no possibility of bailing oneself out of a condition of lostness through human efforts alone. The agency of the adult human being—the ability to recover on one's own strength from the condition of separation from the known—is missing from the discourse.

Even more important, we should note the connection between the condition of lostness, with its psychological correlates, and the condition of victimization that follows. Note how the speech of the excerpt flows seamlessly from a discussion of separation and solitariness to a description of the state of being unprotected and thus easy prey for danger. To set out from the familiar is to get lost; to be lost is to be terrified; to be lost and terrified is to be exposed; to be exposed is to be victimized. The argument is laid out as a series of equations, each outcome following inevitably from the preceding one. To participate in the world on its own terms, without benefit of a life course under the governance of God, is to purchase a horrifying, and malevolent, package deal.

Human Being as Victim

Whence cometh the evils that victimize the wanderer? Let us look once again at the passage in the sermon just examined:

> So many times that's the way man does it. Then he wakes up all alone. He may be in a crowd, but he's all alone. . . . Have you seen stories of the young girls that wander off, leave home, bright lights, dreams of an acting career or a modeling career, and they end up on some strip of prostitution. Victims, dreams tossed aside. [SB]

Note the parallels between the example of the young girls turned prostitute and the child who becomes lost in the department store. In both cases, the victim is an innocent: not an evil nature, but naivete about the ways of the world combined with misguided desires, leads to the wretched outcome. Just as the child becomes lost because of the allure of goods in the department store, so the young girls venture out on the shallow appeal of worldly glamour. They do not understanding how the world treats those who leave the confines of the familiar. The lesson here is that evil lurks everywhere in the world and shows no mercy. There is no protection from the omnipresence of evil, even for the innocent, other than the "correct" conception of God.

What, then, is the source of evil? At first glance, it may seem to come from other, degraded, human beings; prostitutes, of course, cannot ply their trade without their johns. But just as in this sermon there is no sense of human agency for alleviating one's troubles, so there is no notion of human agency for evil. It is not other people who victimize the young girls and turn them into prostitutes; the example is peculiarly depersonalized. The narrative ow of the example focuses on two elements: the innocence of the girls, and their outcome as victims. That others participate in experiences leading to the girls' downfall goes unmentioned, as if to suggest that their role is not the causal one.

Nor, in the sermons portraying the world as a place of terror, is it usually Satan who is the source of evil. In all the sermons we have examined so far, there is only one mention of Satan's agency. One pastor says, in the "call to action" that closes his sermon:

What matters today is that you come home. That you see that without Jesus Christ in your life you're lost. You have no purpose, you have no meaning. You're being kicked around, you're a victim of whatever easy prey Satan might want to pose on you. [SB]

Instead, it is far more commonly suggested that it is the *world*, without benefit of human or supernatural agency, that victimizes people. A symbol that frequently appears in service of this message is the emblem of the unmarked road: the rural byway, without traffic lights or destination signs, used by travelers who are not sure where they are going. Sometimes the lack of signposts leads to temporary misfortune, as an early warning that following an uncharted course will lead to danger. One pastor preaches:

As a student at —— College, we would travel that 20 hour trip before the interstate highway system [was built]. One Sunday night we were heading back after a holiday. There were four or five of us in the car, and one of my roommates was driving. There was a confusing detour sign, and the next thing I remember was waking up in a pasture. What had happened is that my roommate had gotten drowsy, too. He ended up in a pasture because he had missed the right marks, the right signs. We were lost. [SB]

In other cases, the trip down the unmarked road is so risky that it becomes the final voyage. Another pastor tells this story:

I read about an experience in Texas where two main intersections crossed. One main road had a stop sign on both sides of the road. One day a storm blew down the stop sign and it fell in the ditch. It was not long before a family was traveling down this road. But when they arrived at this unfamiliar intersection, and not knowing this was a major intersection where they were supposed to stop, they traveled right on through. They were struck by a truck and killed. [SB]

The outcome of this minatory tale is, of course, predictable from the first sentence. The complexity of the world (symbolized by the intersection) leads to disaster for those who do not see, or do not have access to, the appropriate guidance for navigating it (symbolized by the stop sign). It matters not at all that the travelers are both ignorant and innocent; their fate is guaranteed by the very act of journeying forth from the safety of familiarity. Thus the world makes victims of those foolish enough to trust its ways.

THE WORLD AS PIGPEN

The final category of imagery is that of the world as a place of defilement, a pigpen for the sin and evil habits of the unredeemed. This category appears in 20 percent of the Southern Baptist sermons.[8] In this speech, life on earth is contained in two unmeshed units—the spiritually elevated arena of believers, whose membership in the community of "righteous living" limits their encounter with the defiled world outside; and the much larger realm of the unredeemed, who, in their romp over the natural world, transgress the regulations given by God. Through their transgression, the world is transformed into an evil playground. One's only hope is to cut a wide swath around it.

One pastor equates the contemporary world with the prodigal son's experience of the far country. Although Jesus said little to characterize that alien land, the contemporary Gomorrah is described in detail. Note how the language of this pastor suggests, through its tinges of anachronism and unqualified extremity, that faithfulness to the facts of empirical reality is beside the point. For there can be no concessions in this discourse, no halfway measures; the rhetoric must contain the world and bar entry to it. Barriers are erected in part through the way in which the speech summons up every "devil word" that could be obtained in this context, stringing them together and spitting them out, with the force of curse and incantation:

> The population of the far country is increasing in momentous proportions. Sodom, nude, vile, obscene, filthy and corrupt, demon-possessed in psychedelic debauchery, is about to take over. "Far Country" is just an old way of saying "way out," and America is the farthest out it has ever been. [SB]

The pastor also provides us with a description of the evil conduct of the enemy. One will obviously note the lack of sympathy with which those who inhabit the world are described (in contrast to the stance of all the other sets of sermons). Even though the possibility of demonic possession is implied, the motivations for the deeds of the worldly people are all too clear. They are deliberately attempting to flee from truths that even they can see in their complete transparency. In this speech, the problem with the world is not one of achieving balance, meaning, or safety; these are only superficial issues, since the real problem is the impossibility of achieving righteousness through and in the world. As one pastor says:

> Behold them draped over bars, in the cocktail parties, watching the vileness of Sodom in their living rooms, trying to escape reality with cocaine. The consumption of mental and moral hog food is at an all-time high. The hogs who were demon-possessed at Gadara committed suicide. Mankind should learn that swine would rather die than live like that. [SB]

Note that the boundaries constructed between the world and the true Christian are, in part, effected by a rather diverse catalogue of worldly escape mechanisms. Not only alcohol and drugs, but also television-watching ("the vileness of Sodom in their living rooms") are deemed worldly and sinful conduct. There can be no compromise here between the Christian life and the ways of the world.

As one pastor puts it:

> The world does allure us, they blink their lights at us, and they say to us, we will do this and that for you, and we will make life kind to you. And we're so gullible that we believe that. [SB]

But the siren call of the world leads only to spiritual and even physical death.

CONCLUSIONS

Theorists have speculated that the pluralism of contemporary culture poses serious problems for religious speakers. No longer can churches rely on adherence as a matter of tradition. As plausibility structures weaken for formerly taken-for-granted religious behaviors—as multiple options for belief and allegiance become available—the churches are forced to mount persuasive replies to the offerings of modern times. In the most accommodated response, representing the majority of Presbyterians in the sample, the world of choices poses no difficulty for Christian life, largely because the demands of spirituality are so bounded, so domesticated to concerns of daily middle-class existence, that they do not require abandoning secular pursuits. Thus, an appropriately Christian experience may open itself up to a variety of activities and pleasures of the world. Using the language of humanistic psychology, the pastors teach that faith enriches, rather than conflicts with, ordinary behavior in the world. As I have noted, this response is made possible by the optimistic attitude taken toward the natural and social worlds: that they are benign, under human control.

Southern Baptist responses are more varied, but all are closer to the pole of resistance than to the pole of accommodation. The most extreme response of resistance is made in a small category of speech that proscribes concession by Christians to contemporary secular culture. The prevalent attitude is contempt both for the world of choices and for those who live in it; the speech works to contain the community of the redeemed, sealing symbolic boundaries around it, so that it cannot make polluting contact with the world.

Two other categories occupy the middle ground between the extremes of accommodation and resistance. The first, closer to the Presbyterian response in the way it depicts people's competence to deal with the complexities of modern life, reframes the problem of the secular world from that of sin to that of a deficit of meaning. We have seen how this speech suggests that anxiety over meaninglessness—not over the consequences of sinfulness—is the cross borne by contemporary man. Embracing the options of the mundane world does not end in pollution, as in the most resistant response, but in the far more genteel consequence of emptiness and frustration.

The final set of responses positions itself closer to the stance of world-rejection, as it depicts the secular world of choices neither as opportunity nor as unnecessary and unsatisfying dalliance, but as a place of danger, in which one may lose one's way amid confusions. Yet, in so doing, it speaks realistically to most modern people in acknowledging the temptations of secularity's pluralism. Its response is not castigation but a sympathetic offering of a ticket "home."

Images and Mitigations of Sin

Vengeance is mine, and recompense,
For the time when their foot shall skip;
for the day of their calamity is at hand,
and their doom comes swiftly.
(*Deuteronomy 32:35, Revised Standard Version*)

In the year 1741, while on a visit to the peaceful Connecticut Valley town of Infield, the theologian Jonathan Edwards delivered one of the most unsettling sermons in American history. His message, titled "Sinners in the Hands of an Angry God," explicated the text of Deuteronomy 32:35. Edwards preached:

> The God that holds you over the pit of hell, much as one holds a spider, or some loathsome insect over the re, abhors you, and is dreadfully provoked: his wrath toward you burns like re; he looks upon you as worthy of nothing else, but to be cast into the re; he is of purer eyes than to bear to have you in his sight; you are ten thousand times more abominable in his eyes than the most hateful venomous serpent is in ours. . . . O sinner! Consider the fearful danger you are in: it is a great furnace of wrath, a wide and bottomless pit, full of the re of wrath, that you are held over in the hand of that God, whose wrath is provoked and incensed as much against you, as against many of the damned in hell. [1]

Edwards' sermon is one of the richest depictions of sin and hellfire in popular Protestant preaching in the United States. His elaboration of God's wrath emphasizes the utter separation between the righteous God and the sinful human being, and dramatizes the feelings of guilt and terror that sinful people should feel, Edwards believed, as a result of their fallen state. This message belongs in the context of the First Great Awakening, a powerful revivalist episode in American Protestant history. The movement married revival of Calvinistic teachings about the innate depravity of humankind to urgent exhortations to mass audiences to turn from sin and await the conversion that depends on God's grace. Under the influence of such preachers as Edwards,

George Whitefield, and Gilbert Tennent, hundreds of men and women became convinced of the need to seek salvation.[2]

But just as the image of God has undergone change over the course of the American Protestant experience, so has the conception of sin and its meaning for humankind. Revival of the stark Calvinist doctrine of human depravity and God's "irresistible grace" during the First Great Awakening was relatively short-lived. The experience of American colonists during the Revolutionary War helped popularize concepts of liberty, individualism, voluntarism, and democracy, sentiments which, on the level of common sense, appeared to falsify Calvinist teachings. In particular, Calvinist doctrines of humankind's innate and utter sinfulness, salvation only of the elect, and God's total control over the process of conversion came under attack.[3] By the time of the Second Great Awakening, early in the nineteenth century, evangelists such as Charles Finney were preaching doctrines that emphasized a person's free will to seek salvation and the assurance of that salvation immediately upon repentance. No longer was it necessary for those experiencing the "conviction of their sins" to wait, in suffering silence, upon God's will.[4] By the end of the nineteenth century, the Calvinist doctrine of predestination had been rejected by most segments of American Protestantism, and the doctrine of human depravity was on the wane. The conversion event, spurred on by the long experience of revivalism, took on heightened importance, but it became transmuted in some quarters into a process partially under human control. The active syntax of "deciding to be saved" was heard alongside more traditional notions of human beings as vehicles for God's deed of salvation.[5]

The ideas of human sinfulness and the need for salvation were fundamental components—indeed, theological motives—for the revivals. But the concept of sin underwent a transformation in some quarters of Protestantism, including Presbyterianism in the northern states, as the result of a massive reinterpretation of Christian purpose during the mid- and late-nineteenth century. The reinterpretation entailed three related changes: the rejection of determinism as a result of the rise of positivism, evident in scientific research and biblical criticism; an emphasis on Arminian doctrines of free will; and a tendency toward optimism about the good in human nature.[6] As a result, the Calvinist doctrine of original sin was transformed, by some groups, into notions of sin as mistakes in behavior, amenable to correction by appropriate education.[7]

Liberal optimism about the human condition, especially with respect to the ability of human beings to "do something" to correct their own sin, did not go unchallenged. In the late nineteenth and early twentieth centuries, two countermovements arose with a compelling theological retort to liberal Christianity. The fundamentalist response, among other things, reappropriated the doctrine of the essential sinfulness of humankind, in particular denying the ability of human beings to solve the problem of sin through their own efforts.[8] And neo-orthodoxy formulated a theologically sophisticated critique of optimistic, "this-worldly" liberal Protestantism, emphasizing the majesty and transcendence of God and the depths of human sinfulness.[9]

Sin in Contemporary Context

How does the idea of sin fare in the sermons under study here? We should not be surprised to find that communicating notions of sin poses difficulties for many of the pastors.[10] For of all of the theological topics on which the Parable of the Prodigal Son invites discussion, probably none is potentially more distasteful to modern sensibilities than traditional notions of sin and its eternal consequences for those who are not "saved." These theological teachings premise serious limitations on both human capabilities for action and human understanding that fly in the face of our most pronounced secular ideologies.

These ideologies include the pervasive motifs of humanistic psychology, the myths of rugged individualism and the "self-crafted self," and the rational, pragmatic bent that characterizes behavior in business and public life. They focus attention on people's abilities to control their own lives, on purposive action in the here-and-now, and on the human capacity for autonomy, self-awareness, and self-development.

Set against these cultural themes are theological notions that tell people that they are by nature likely to sin, that some of the norms validated by secular culture are actually sin, that they will have to account for their behavior to an unseen, all-powerful God who surpasses human comprehension, and that they will meet their reward or suffer punishment in an unverifiable realm called the "afterlife" that is, contrary to every thread of commonsense experience, what the game is said to be all about.

Confronting the dilemma of speaking about sin in a secular age, preachers have a variety of options. At the extremes lie the strongest positions of resistance or accommodation. The former is effected by ignoring, debunking, or constructing discursive disconfirmations of secular ideologies; the latter works as speakers fully adjust religious concepts to consonance with secular modes of thought, while eliminating or naturalizing troublesome notions in one's talk. As I examine the sermons, I note a few examples of the first strategy (from Southern Baptist speakers who cleave to traditional formulations) and rather more of the second (from Presbyterian speakers who reinterpret sin as misguided behavior, removed from theological grounding). But there is also a vast middle road available to speakers, and it is upon this road that most of the preachers steer: asserting traditional concepts of sin and its consequences but with the rhetorical demeanor of a softened, genteel, and inoffensive style of speech called civility.

In his study of contemporary evangelicalism, James Hunter describes some aspects of the civil style of discourse.[11] The overall message, he writes, is that of "no offense";[12] speakers take care to frame potentially distasteful messages so as to cushion their negative effects. Hunter finds that notions of sin and its consequences are likely to be discussed in abstract and indirect terms. Talk about sin is generalized, and no specific individuals or groups of people are targeted as objects of the message. Further, speakers suggest a degree of tolerance for the beliefs and practices of others. We shall see some of these strategies displayed in the speech of the sermons, but there are also others that I shall identify; the sermons use an impressive array of creative rhetorical devices to deflect the force of notions of sinfulness from "zinging home" (as one preacher puts it) to their audiences.

Depicting the Parable Characters

In exploring how the speakers talk about sin through their interpretation of the behavior of the two scriptural brothers, we shall note, as we might expect, marked differences between the two denominations. (Southern Baptist speakers are more likely than Presbyterians to treat the topic of sin at all in these sermons; the topic appears in all the Southern Baptist sermons, but in only half of the Presbyterian texts.) For Southern Baptists, with their self-conscious charge to evangelism, it is the younger son, bottomed out in the pigpen, whose behavior is the dramatic negative example. Indeed, *dramatic* is the operative word here; Southern Baptist pastors are likely to offer graphic, urgent depictions of the young man's downfall. He is described as a youth in the throes of adolescent revolt against the will of his father, seen in the sermons as the conscious motivation for his behavior. The son's actions of demanding his inheritance before it is due, leaving home to seek his own life, and experiencing riotous living in the far country are viewed as clear examples of sin in its biblical sense of rebellion. Thus one preacher describes the son, stressing the deliberately antiauthoritarian messages he is sending his father:

> He rebelled against the father and the home. He was saying by what he was doing that home wasn't good enough for him, he was saying by his actions that they [his family] weren't considerate enough of him, he was saying by what choices he made that "I can make it better on my own than I can make it here." [SB]

Indeed, for some pastors, the sin of the prodigal son is the ultimate transgression, for they read the son's untimely demand for his inheritance not only as the subversion of appropriate relationships of authority, but also as a symbolic act of patricide. In a formulation echoed in several other sermons, this speaker dramatizes the murderous aim of the son:

> [The prodigal son] goes to his father and he's not only making a request for money, he's really saying, "Dad, I wish you were dead. Right now, and I had the money, and I could go on with my life." [SB]

The behavior of the younger brother is especially odious, in this talk, precisely because it is deliberate. These speakers suggest that the son's rebellion against authority is carefully planned, motivated by the evil intentions of selfishness and disrespect. We shall see below that many Presbyterian pastors account for the behavior of this boy in far gentler terms. Here, however, there is no escape for the younger brother, as most Southern Baptist speakers place blame for the sinful deeds squarely on his shoulders. As one pastor preaches, emphasizing the greediness and arrogance of the son's actions:

> The younger son was covetous. And even though he had no right to demand it, he walked up to his father according to verse 12 and said, "Father, give me the portion of goods that falleth to me." . . . [The son] does not even exercise the ethical standards by which we ought to live, and say to him, "please, father, give me this chance." . . . But instead he walked up to his father very arrogantly and he demands of his father that which he says is my right. [SB]

As if rebellion and symbolic patricide were not enough to heap judgment on the son's head, many of the Southern Baptist preachers elabo-

83

rate further on the significance of his sin. It is the lever that pries open the lid on the Pandora's box of further sinful behavior. In the excerpt below, rebellion against the father is only the beginning of an inevitable career of sin; once the boy leaves home, sin follows on the heels of sin. Note how events in this process are tied together by short, grammatically equivalent clauses:

> It is obvious to all of us why the younger son would be labelled a sinner, for he openly rebelled against his father, wasted his father's money, ran with a fast crowd, fell into every conceivable kind of immorality, and ended up a physical and spiritual wreck. [SB]

For another pastor, likewise, the act of rebellion is merely the edge of the quagmire of sin and self-destruction. In this passage, the point of origin for the downslide into sin is distinctly marked:

> This young man when he asked for everything and as you'll notice in the text it says it took him a few days before he left town. In the very beginning when he says "give me what is mine," at that very moment [his] life has been injured but from that point on [his] life began to be wasted. And all the resources that God gave to him are one by one squandered away. [SB]

In the next excerpt, the sins of the younger brother appear as a series of steps away from God. Here, too, one step follows directly from another, as after rebellion comes:

> the natural consequence, and that is, . . . wickedness. . . . He became involved in wickedness. If you read the verses of Scripture that follow the verses we read, you would know from the elder son, the brother of this wayward son, you would know what he has done. . . . "He has devoured your living with harlots.". . . He became involved in wicked living. There aren't many steps from the time you begin to demand your rights and you begin to want your own and you begin to become covetous and rebellious against authority. There aren't many steps until you find yourself down in the pigpen, down in the far country, down in the place where the world lives in its filthiness. [SB]

Down in the pigpen. This is the final step in the process of degradation. Because, in this talk, no behavior is discrete or inconsequential, the eventual result of rebellion and wickedness is the destruction of the young man's dignity and self-respect, the degradation of his personality. As we shall see in chapter six, Southern Baptists place the positive qualities of dignity and self-respect at the center of the essential, God-given self. For now, it suffices to note that, as they posit the young man's self-destruction, these preachers are depicting the depths of the abyss into which sin has flung the boy. As the sermons imply, the son's sin has violated him in three ways, all of which demolish his human dignity: by subjecting him to a state of hunger so extreme that he is desperate for the food of animals; by the breaking of religious princi-ple, which opens him up to the abhorrent task of tending pigs; and by the physical effects of sin which inevitably follow from his actions.[13] For he wears the effects of his rebellion on his sleeve, so to speak; in order to dramatize the worldly wages of sin, speakers describe the bod-ily marks of the young man's sinful behavior. One pastor says:

> The Bible says that the father was out there looking for [the son]. The father recognized his step, and even though he didn't look like the boy that went away, even though his clothes were rags and even though he was stooped over and all of the effects of the rebellion were show-ing in his life, there was something about his step that the father recog-nized. [SB]

But these portraits of the prodigal son's downfall, pathetic as they are, are emphatically not meant to inspire pity. The speakers make it clear that the young man has earned his degradation. They read it as an unambiguous illustration of the biblical principle that, "As a man sows, so shall he reap." One pastor makes an issue of the emotions one should properly feel for the boy, marking it with the phrase, "I want to tell you something":

> The boy is in trouble and he probably is miserable. I want to tell you something. He's only getting what he deserves. And you ought not to waste your sympathy on him. There is something terribly wrong with that boy. [SB]

The younger brother's behavior, then, is so dramatic an emblem of sin to Southern Baptists not only because it symbolizes violation of the key relationship of authority—that between child and parent, and by extension, people and God—but also because it leads the son down the slippery slope of sin culminating in the degradation of the human per-sonality. To begin the slide through an act of rebellion is eventually to find the muck of the swine at one's feet.

For Presbyterian speakers, on the other hand, it is the dutiful, reli-giously obedient, yet joyless older brother who is more likely to serve as the emblem of sin. This man has two major strikes against him: He is full of self-righteousness about his own dutiful behavior, and he lacks sufficient charity to welcome his errant brother home. Some speakers add a further litany of sins to the catalogue. For example, in one sermon, the older brother is seen as guilty of:

> subtle sins of envy, prejudice, bad temper, self-centeredness, a judgmental attitude, criticizing everybody in sight, and a lack of love! [P]

In general, however, the older son is found blameworthy because his moral self-righteousness leads him to judge his own worth as greater than that of his brother. He cannot understand why this fact should not be self-evident to his father. These assumptions lead to nastiness, sulking, and a refusal to be happy that his brother has returned. These sins are subtle, the sermons suggest, but no less to be shunned than outright rebellion. As one pastor says:

> I believe that the parable is saying that being self-centered, righteous, and unforgiving is just as sinful as waywardness and rebellion. [P]

Another preacher furthers this theme, and links it to the older brother's unpleasant personality:

> The older son comes home, finds a feast going on, he begins to pout and refuses to come in. When we look at sin, not theologically, but in its everyday clothes, we find two kinds. You find sins of passion and sins of temper. The sins of passion are all the forms of lust and selfishness. The sins of temper are all the forms of pride and anger. We tend to judge the sins of passion more harshly. But you might ask whether we conceal beneath respectable, moral exteriors, the spirit of the older brother, the sulky, self-righteousness of a rotten temperament. [P]

In the following excerpt, a pastor links the older brother's jealousy of his sibling to hypocrisy. The older brother pretends to be dutifully religious, but a truly religious person would understand that he should feel joy when a sinner repents:

> Here we see the life-size portrait of a dull saint. He was self-righteous. The holier-than-thou is always jealous. He was even jealous of his brother's repentance . . . [he] pretended to worship God . . . in actuality, he is his own god worshipping himself. This dull saint was 100 percent synthetic. [P]

What is accomplished in these portraits of the sin of the older brother? It appears that, for these speakers, there is no slide into sin, no dramatic trajectory. Unlike the urgent momentum of Southern Baptist depictions of the prodigal son's downfall, in Presbyterian portraits, the older brother's acts of self-righteousness and lack of charity are discrete and independent of other behavior. The older brother simply remains outside the party, performing his chores with a nasty pout. In these images, his behavior appears to have no consequences for others, nor even, beyond his rigid personality, for himself.

Also, note that the portraits are internalized and psychologized. Whereas the younger brother's sins are dramatized in terms of an external, visible effect, these depictions highlight the personality of the older brother instead of the result of his behavior. Here, sin is a matter of temperament and personality, of having the wrong attitude, of not feeling the appropriate emotions in one's heart and acting on the feelings, rather than of dramatic antiauthoritarian behavior and its effects. Finally, the speakers in this group of sermons appear far less harsh in passing judgments on the older brother's sin than do the Southern Baptists concerning the sin of the prodigal son, as the older brother's sin is attributed to a nasty temperament or a "synthetic" self, is deemed error, or is barely elaborated upon.

Generalizing Sin

The sermons do not, of course, confine their comments on sin to interpretation of the scriptural characters. They also generalize to larger contexts of meaning. Generalization is accomplished through two types of formulations: propositional claims and exemplification. In the first, speakers render and explain doctrine; in the second, the idea of sin is given flesh through characters inserted in stories and commentaries.

The large majority of the Southern Baptist pastors (75 percent) and a small fraction of Presbyterians (11 percent) state at least once in their sermons the doctrine of the universality of sin: that no human being, with the exception of Jesus Christ, is exempt from sin. Evidence for this proposition is sometimes given by prooftext. Updating Paul's theological language (Romans 3:23), one pastor draws upon the lyrics of country and western music:

> The Bible says all have sinned and fallen short of the glory of God. That means that we are living our lives away from God and we have committed so many sins that we are like the guy coming home to his

girl from prison . . . [in the] story of "Tie a Yellow Ribbon Round the Old Oak Tree." [SB]

Another preacher links the doctrine both to the text of the Lost Sheep that precedes the Parable of the Prodigal Son and to Isaiah 53:6:

Like the Bible says, all we like sheep have gone astray. [SB]

More frequently, speakers ground the proposition in an analogy with the behavior of the prodigal son. Since, it is assumed, the son's conduct obviously is sinful, and since it is assumed that Jesus told the parable in order to make a general point about human nature, the conclusion is inescapable that all are sinners. For example, as he introduces his narrative paraphrase of the first half of the parable, this preacher says:

I've wondered if perhaps Jesus knew these two sons; if perhaps He turned a local situation into a parable that says for all time that all men are prodigal sons in some way—all have journeyed into a far country—all have chosen away from the father and have need to draw close to him again. [SB]

Another Southern Baptist echoes this formulation:

You know, all of us have in our own way repeated the story of this wayward boy. We were the special creation of God and the whole earth was ours to enjoy. But selfish desire led us all to leave our heavenly father. [SB]

Propositional claims suggesting universal sinfulness are not conned to Southern Baptists. Some Presbyterian speakers also propose that the behavior of the prodigal son is sinful, then analogize outward to all humankind. But the claim that all are sinners apparently causes some trouble for these speakers; it requires a more cautious approach. One pastor eases into the equation; note the foot-in-the door strategy where assent is sought incrementally, as the talk builds toward an assertion of universal sinfulness:

The younger son [sinned] because he didn't want to do what was expected of him—he wanted to be free and independent. Doesn't this sound familiar? I'm sure we wouldn't have to think too hard before we could name someone who has this same adventurous spirit. It's probably safe to say that most of us at one time or another have decided that we're going to do something our way. All of us are prodigal sons and daughters. [P]

Another Presbyterian pastor demands that all people see themselves in the behavior of the young man, although he concedes that the recognition might be grudging and painful. The following story appears in the context of the preacher's description of the prodigal son's sin:

> Helmut Thielike relates the story out of his own family experience that is very similar to ones we have had. He tells of his young son for the first time looking into a mirror. And as he looked into the mirror, the son seemed to show absolutely no recognition at all that the little fellow in the mirror could be himself. Slowly it seemed to dawn upon him that the person moving there was actually a reflection. And so it is with us as we look at this parable. When first we read it or hear it, we may think that there is nothing of ourselves in it. But then we discover the parable is indeed reading us. [P]

In their propositions, then, many of the speakers seem to have retained some of the traditional force of notions of sin, communicating a sense that human sinfulness is inescapable. But two devices of civility are already visible here that modify the force of this doctrine. These devices shield listeners from the harshness of direct identification, as if the pastors were saying, "When we talk about sinners, well, yes, you're probably included, but we are not particularly pointing the finger at *you*."

First is the device of depersonalization, which flattens and defuses the effect of the idea of the sinner in talk about the universality of sin. In naming the doctrine, speakers take care to encode human beings in the collective "we," or even more weakly, "all men," instead of using rhetorical formulations that could personalize the accusation of sin to individual human beings.

Second is the device of selectivity, which works to omit mentions of causality for sin. The doctrine of the universality of sin loses much of its bite, since little note is taken of the *source* of human beings' tendency toward transgression: Adam's fall, the generation of original sin. We have already seen how this doctrine might be especially distasteful to modern listeners, since it assumes that human beings lack control over their behavior when it comes to their inherited tendency to sin.

But these rhetorical formulations provide only minor strategies compared to a third set of devices, which allow speakers to articulate a doctrine of sin while at the same time palliating the harshness of its application to the listening audience. These devices operate as speakers exemplify sin, in the little stories they tell, through characters other than the brothers of the parable. The first is the rhetorical device of deflection: It works by projecting sin away from the listening audience and onto specific groups of outsiders.

Deflecting Sin to Outsiders

Twenty sermons contain examples of specific, contemporary human beings in concrete acts of sin. Eleven of the stories thus describe children. Children are wonderfully apt exemplars of sin, within the framework of these sermons, for several reasons. They are relevant to the parable (most speakers portray the younger brother as a late teenager or young adult, not as a grown man); when sin is described as "rebellion," the ordinary conduct of children seems obviously to fit the definition; their behavior is highly salient, since they are ours and we are responsible for them; yet they are not Us—they are clearly Other.

As one pastor puts it, in a formulation that suggests the universal parental experience of bafflement and frustration at the alien qualities of children's personalities, the tenacity and irrationality of their will:

> Did you ever try to reason with a child, who had determined in his mind what he was going to do, and who said, as they often do, "Don't confuse me with the facts, my mind is already made up. I'm going to do this thing, or die doing it." Did you ever try to reason with a child who wanted ice cream or candy, who wanted to wear a certain dress or pair of pants or a shirt, who wanted to go to a certain place and you said no? Did you ever try to reason with them, and tell them all the logic that's involved in the decisions you made for them? They don't hear any of it. [SB]

Another pastor decries the epidemic of adolescent rebellion, a byproduct, he says, of children's selfish natures:

> I believe the root cause of [sin] is the rebelliousness that young people have against their parents. And the wastefulness of the youth generation that we see, where we see wastefulness, it is the result of saying "no" to parents and saying "give me, give me, give me." And it has destroyed their lives. [SB]

Several speakers have anecdotes to tell of their own childhood sin, as if to emphasize the breadth of the distance between the uncorrected child and the corrected adult, yet to provide direct evidence of the possibilities of conversion (even such a miscreant as this can become a Christian—and not only that, but an actual preacher). One pastor says:

> I never forget those times when I got mad at home and decided to run away. . . . I would announce to [my father] that I was sick and tired of the way I was being treated and my rights were being trampled upon and I had no freedom and liberty and I was going to leave home. . . . Well, there was in this boy [ambiguously referring both to the prodigal son and to the speaker] a spirit of rebellion in which he turned and walked away from the people who loved him the most. [SB]

Commenting on the obviousness of the notion of children as sinners, while adding fuel to the fire with his own confession, another pastor says:

> I don't need the Bible to tell me, I don't need God to come down from heaven to tell me, that boys sometimes become prodigals. I already knew that. I was one and I had one. And I found that out on my own, and by the way while I'm at it I might as well say that not all prodigals are boys. [SB]

This preacher offers a dramatic account of his own adolescent sin and its visible effects:

> I'm not sure I've shared this with you, but on my forearms, on both arms, there are two scars, burns. Two separate accidents when I was a teenager. Two times of disobedience, two burns. . . . I could take my hand and through my very coat I can trace those scars. I live the experience, I remember the consequences. Sin will always leave a scar. [SB]

A second small category of imagery around the concrete identification of sinners concerns people whose outré behavior marks them as members of a diseased secular world (there are seven examples). In most cases, the behavior is so outrageous within the context of community norms that the examples serve more as symbols demarcating Them from Us than as practical warning about potential conduct. Drug abuse, alcoholism, compulsive gambling, murder, and prostitution are usually cited. Some notations of sin and sinners are quite explicit, as in this excerpt:

> Behold them draped over bars, in the cocktail parties, watching the vileness of Sodom in their living rooms, trying to escape reality with cocaine. The consumption of mental and moral hog food is at an all-time high. The hogs who were demon-possessed at Gadara committed

suicide. Mankind should learn that swine would rather die than live like that. [SB]

A few sermons set up as sinful the behavior of specific social groups. One preacher thus labels the poor and racial/ethnic minorities, through a list that equates people in these categories with those who are spiritually "sick" (beer drinkers and divorced people):

Who do you visit on Tuesday visitation? Jesus said, "They that be whole need not a physician." Yet most of our time and ministry goes to those who are not sick, while we shy away from the poor, the blacks, the Hispanics, the beer drinkers, and the divorced. [SB]

And another speaker clearly identifies a social underclass for whom one should have compassion, namely:

Criminals, prostitutes, addicts, homosexuals, the obese, the ugly, and the different. [SB]

Yet another displacement of charges of sin onto groups other than one's own occurs around the category of Jews (there are eight instances). Certainly, the Parable of the Prodigal Son, and other gospel texts, extend an invitation to view the Pharisees as wrongdoers. In particular, the character of the older brother offers speakers the narrative type of the Pharisee to criticize.[14] But in the sermons, commentaries on Jewish sinfulness are not always limited to the context of Jesus' day.

As background for notions of Jewish sinfulness is the constitution of the Jew as the incomprehensible stranger. In this small category, Jews behave in ways that their Christian colleagues find peculiar, alien, and irrational. One pastor tells this story as an aside to his exposition of the prodigal son's job in the pigpen; in a sermon with no other digressions, the appearance of the story is surprising:

I recall taking a Jewish Christian brother out for a meal years ago. . . . When the food arrived, he was horrified to find that it had bacon in the sandwich. He called the waitress and asked her to take it away. [My wife] and I were somewhat embarrassed, but he explained that even as a Christian he could not escape his Jewish revulsion at eating any part of a pig. Personally I can't stand liver, although there is nothing religious behind my feelings. At least his scruples had an historical basis. [P]

The equation made here between the cultural taboos of Jewish dietary laws and personal taste regarding food sets up the fuss made by the guest as unnecessary, inappropriate, and inexplicable. Even the concession that "his scruples had an historical basis" tends to trivialize the quality of Jewish observance into an arbitrary piece of conduct by not acknowledging the forceful social and religious context of the dietary norms. Furthermore, despite the reference to the guest as a "brother," the story implies, "It just goes to show you—once a Jew, always a Jew," laying boundaries around the category of Jew as Other.

The second example is broader in focus, but certainly includes Jews as prime candidates for its charge. It is a rather softened variation on the age-old theme of the culpable stubbornness of Jewish resistance to conversion. In this discourse, Jews, like others who reject Christ, are merely crazy. But craziness is not altogether innocent, in this speech, for a disordered mental state, like that of the prodigal son when he left home, is likely to express itself in rebellion and sin. Speaking of the contrasting qualities of the prodigal son's mind before and after he came to himself, and elaborating on the mental balance of people before they convert, one preacher says:

> This is true. It's absolute truth. No person who lives his life without acknowledging and believing in Jesus Christ is of sane mind. [SB]

Other speakers make more explicit links between Jews and sin by drawing an analogy between Jews and the older brother of the parable. With one exception, these analogies are limited to the Jews of Jesus' day or to those who declined to accept his divinity during the apostolic era. A Presbyterian pastor says:

> The parable warns . . . how Paul indicated to the Jews who rejected Christ, that God had rejected them unless they too should repent. [P]

Another preacher reads the entire parable typologically, with Jews as the self-righteous and unforgiving older brother:

> I believe the two sons represent the prideful Israel and the gentile world out there and that the world could come back to God no matter what they'd done yet the prideful Jewish people did not like it that He was receiving sinners and He was reminding them through these two sons that God received anybody who has a repentant heart. [SB]

The following excerpt is more ambiguous about limiting the identification of sinners to the ancient Jews, as, again, a connection is made between the Jews and the older brother:

[The older brother] never saw the significance in the empty chairs at his Father's table—chairs for publicans and sinners . . . I often wondered why the brother didn't ask about the empty chair; maybe he didn't ask because he didn't want to look for him; maybe because he didn't want to share the limelight, or the wealth, or the position, or anything else. Israel, God's chosen people, responded in just such a fashion! [SB]

The one exception mentioned above—which appears to make a link between the modern Jew and sin—is found in the next excerpt. The sermon from which it is drawn is one of the few from Presbyterian speakers that is relatively strong on the idea of sin; for this pastor, the older brother serves to exemplify the notion of sinfulness. Here, the sinful qualities of the older brother—his lack of forgiveness for a brother who had wronged him—appear to be equated with the failure of a contemporary Jew, who is a prisoner in a Nazi concentration camp, to offer his forgiveness to a dying SS trooper. (I have summarized parts of the narrative elaboration in brackets, but have reproduced the speaker's commentary in full):

The fatal flaw in [the older brother] was the sin of disposition. He had no capacity to love, to forgive! Simon Wiesenthal was an architect by profession, but because he was Jewish he was caught up in the Nazi domination of Poland, and found himself . . . in a concentration camp.

One day [while working in the camp's hospital], he was summoned by a nurse to the bedside of a fatally wounded SS trooper. The trooper looked at him and in a kind of desperation and catharsis of confession began to pour out this story of his need to talk to a Jew. He said that in a village as his army was moving they packed two hundred Jews into a small house that they had soaked with gasoline . . . and then threw a hand grenade in and it burst into flames. [The dying trooper then tells a heartrending tale of a mother and baby attempting to escape the house by jumping out a window. The trooper tells of shooting the mother and child to death.] Then the trooper said, "I know that what I have told you is terrible. I have longed to talk about it to a Jew and beg forgiveness from him. I know that what I am asking is almost too much, but without your answer I cannot die in peace."

And Wiesenthal tells us what he did. 'I stood up and looked in his direction, at his folded hands. At last I made up my mind and without a word I left the room.'

The German soldier went to his destiny unforgiven by man! Now I am not sure I could have forgiven him, or that any of us could have!

But I know this: that one of the keys to life is in forgiveness, and it is always costly! It cost God His son; it may cost us our pride as we seek His healing and His help! [P]

It is clear here that an identification is being made between the figure of the sinful older brother and the unforgiving Jew, Simon Wiesenthal. The "fatal flaw" of the older brother—his incapacity to love or forgive—is directly and unambiguously linked, both thematically and by juxtaposition, with the failure of Simon Wiesenthal, an inmate in a concentration camp, to grant forgiveness to a Nazi torturer. (The sinful qualities of the older brother are mentioned in the first two sentences; the character of Wiesenthal is introduced without narrative break in the third. And the words "forgive" and "forgiveness" are used to refer to both characters.)

Despite the speaker's demurral that he does not know whether he himself could have forgiven the Nazi or that anyone he is addressing could have done so, the implication is plain that Wiesenthal should have found the higher ground by granting the Nazi his dying wish. Instead, this excerpt implies, Wiesenthal acted according to his Jewish tendencies, seeking justice rather than offering forgiveness. The sermon creates out of Wiesenthal a convenient, contemporary type of the legalistic older brother. For as many Americans are undoubtedly aware, Wiesenthal has become a prominent "Nazi hunter," expending his efforts to ascertain that Nazis be brought to judgment, a mission he publicly justifies through reference to Old Testament moral norms.[15]

MITIGATING THE SINS OF INSIDERS

In addition to deflecting blame for sin away from listeners by telling stories that exemplify others as sinners, the sermons use another rhetorical device to avoid "pointing the finger" at the audience, the device of mitigation. It works this way: When listeners are identified with the prodigal son or with the older brother, the sermons tend to weaken the force of these characters' sinfulness. They do so either by downplaying the severity of the sins of the brothers, or by supplying other, less blameworthy, characters with whom the audience may choose to identify instead.

For example, after he asks his listeners to examine themselves to see whether they might resemble the older brother, one pastor provides this explanation for the brother's behavior:

We could diagnose [the older brother] as being narcissistic. . . . The narcissistic personality disorder was given official clinical status by the American Psychiatric Association in 1980. Dr. Robert L. Spitzer describes the narcissistic person in these terms: He has a grandiose sense of self-importance, and exaggerates his achievements. He is preoccupied with fantasies of unlimited success and greatness. He requires constant attention and affirmation. He usually responds to criticism or defeat with marked feelings of rage. He is further characterized by these two things: a lack of empathy, and entitlement—that is, the expectation of special favors. Isn't that amazing? It is as if Dr. Spitzer was reading the parable of the older brother and giving a clinical diagnosis of him, for that was precisely his problem. [SB]

Aside from mitigating the older brother's responsibility for his behavior by suggesting that it fits the description of a psychiatric disease, surely the diagnosis presented here would preempt any identification by the audience with him. The technical jargon in the definition of narcissism, the portrait of a character not in terms of personality but through the formal criteria of a list, robs the older brother of a concrete identity with whom people can identify even if they were so inclined. In addition, the diagnosis seems comically misguided; only the first item of the last entry—a lack of empathy—seems reasonably to describe the man found in Luke. Thus, the audience is shielded from the sinful man: It is the diagnosis that acts—the depersonalized list of characteristics—not a realistic depiction of the older brother.

In the following excerpt (which we have already seen in another context), an invitation is offered to the audience to identify with the sins of the older brother, but the proposal is cushioned by several layers of indirection and civility:

> When we look at sin, not theologically, but in its everyday clothes, we find two kinds. You find sins of passion and sins of temper. The sins of passion are all the forms of lust and selfishness. The sins of temper are all the forms of pride and anger. We tend to judge the sins of passion more harshly. But you might ask whether we conceal beneath respectable, moral exteriors, the spirit of the older brother, the sulky, self-righteousness of a rotten temperament. [P]

First, we should note that, initially, listeners are given the high ground. They are invited to stand "above" the material, sheltered from accusations of sinfulness by the speaker's inclusion of them in the abstract, detached analysis of the older brother's sin. Then, when the opportunity to identify with the older brother is offered, it is presented in the conditional, rather than the imperative, mode, leaving it up to the listeners to choose the identification if they wish. Further, this talk reduces the sin of the older brother to possession of a nasty personality. The speaker has already conceded that, by implication, the older brother's sins appear less serious than those of the younger son (with whom the pastor does not suggest his audience has anything in common). Yet the final sentence mitigates the older brother's sin even more, even to the vanishing point, where the notion of sin is effectively transmuted into an issue of polite behavior.

Finally, in a masterful stroke, a Southern Baptist preacher shelters his listeners from direct accusation of sinfulness by offering for identification, in place of the blameworthy prodigal son, a rich narrative type that can be called the "Lost Child." This character meanders, in various guises, from one story to another in the sermon. Whether the Lost Child appears in an anecdote about a family outing as the preacher's own toddler who roams off after a baseball game, or as the child whose curiosity leads him to explore a department store alone, or as the college student who unwittingly drives off the highway into a cornfield in the rural South, or as a young country girl who leaves the safety of home for the dangers of the big city, it is essentially the same person. The Lost Child is an innocent, who loses the way by inattention, who strays because of the inherent complexity of the world, who embodies an account of sin as "wandering" or "drifting off the path," for which the sinner is not at fault. And the pastor takes an utterly sympathetic tone to this guileless errancy, modeling for the audience his feelings about the behavior with which he has suggested they identify. In a commentary on the child in the department store, he says:

> We end up in the middle of nowhere and we don't know how to get back. Years of wandering, hoping for something better, always looking for the greener grass on the other side until finally we are so far away from everything that has spiritually been familiar . . . we don't know how to get back. Constantly missing the right path, no evil intended, just wandering. [SB]

THERAPEUTIC TOLERANCE

But for that sizable proportion of speakers in the sample (mainly Presbyterians) for whom devices of deflection and mitigation do not suffice, there is a more extreme device through which to soften notions of sin.

The strategy is exemplified in texts that never refer, even obliquely, to the topic of sin. In these sermons, the behavior of the two brothers is seen as wrong, inviting commentary, even, sometimes, negative evaluation. Unlike the sermons we have seen so far, however, the predominant tendency in these portraits of the two brothers is toward expression of an evenhanded attitude toward their behavior. This stance attempts both to account for the brothers' conduct in terms that are relatively value-free, and to understand, and empathize with, the hurts the brothers are said to cause themselves through their misguided actions. In so doing, the sermons position the listeners (who are invited to identify with the brothers' actions, especially with those of the older brother) as vicarious clients in a mass session of Rogerian therapy, as the talk displays a style of therapeutic warmth, acceptance, and tolerance.

Tolerance, James Hunter writes, accompanies the modern American experience of cultural pluralism, the pressure to accept, or at least allow, the differences of others.[16] It also is a concomitant of the social processes by which religious formulations are demonopolized, religious truths are deobjectified, and religious practices are deinstitutionalized. In the weakening of cognitive certainties, as religious knowledge becomes opinion and conviction becomes preference, as the grounds for religious speech are transferred from the objective to the subjective, the range of acceptable religious belief and practice grows wider. For, on what grounds can one say that a certain religious tenet or particular religious practice is right or wrong? How can one claim to hold a monopoly on the truth, or rule out the possibility that another's formulation is equally justifiable?

If the pastors are reluctant to judge the behavior of the prodigal son, their sympathetic tone is especially pronounced in these sermons about the older brother (who is, after all, a familiar middle-class type: dutiful, hard-working, and respectful of parental authority). In these excerpts, the attitude toward the older brother is one of empathy—the articulation of feelings of regret that his behavior prevents him from realizing the benefits to himself that might otherwise ensue. One pastor speaks of the psychological pain that the brother will continue to suffer as a result of his closed, bitter personality, not as a matter of just deserts, but with the empathic and supportive tone of a practiced humanistic psychologist:

> The older son is still sorting through truth—trying to make some sense
> of what he sees happening. If he keeps searching I'm sure he'll be

freed. But if he gives in to his resentment, nurturing his bitterness, he will become so calloused that truth and joy will have an almost impossible time breaking through. [P]

As another Presbyterian pastor comments on the older brother, his concern is with the limits on "growth" that the man's pessimism will earn him:

The older son chooses to look for the bad in life and chooses to place his hurt feelings first and wastes yet another opportunity to grow in the understanding of the power of love. [P]

For the next speaker, as well, the problem with the older brother is the psychological pain he causes himself. His bitterness keeps him from experiencing the joy of a relationship with God:

It's a tragic thing to be at a celebration and not be able to celebrate. To be a wallower at God's party and not be able to dance and sing. To miss the joy: that's to miss everything! [P]

When they turn to the prodigal son, the pastors call on the resources of social science to give a sympathetic, or at least neutral, gloss to his behavior. First is the family systems approach, as we see in this excerpt:

The younger brother [in a family] . . . cannot manage to find acceptance or approval [through obedience]. . . . They're not big enough, experienced enough, mature enough to compete in such matters with an older brother or sister. But there is an alternative: they can at least get some attention by rebelling. [P]

Here, another pastor provides a family history for the son's departure from home:

We don't know what preceded it, the many family dinners which deteriorated into an intramural contest between siblings, the violent arguments, the incessant challenges to parental authority. Maybe that boy had to go. Maybe there was no way for him to discover who he was and what life is about in the long shadow of his older brother. [P]

Another account is given through the "growth and development" trope. The son isn't sinful, he is just basically juvenile, as we see in this excerpt:

The prodigal was an immature person who ran out of the resources necessary to sustain his immaturity. So when he hit rock bottom he redirected his life toward worthier possibilities. [P]

Or, as in this message, the son is a bit of a reckless Candide, who:

> fell for one of these get-rich-quick schemes that await the naive. He
> was careless of his resources and ran through his inheritance the way
> water runs through open fingers. His plans and intentions were good,
> but he didn't have the experience or maturity to carry them out ...
> There were no real friends, no thoughtful advisors in that far-away
> country. [P]

The sermon excerpt that is most revealing about the grounds for tolerance in this talk opens with a disclaimer:

> I discovered that by trying to name the two young men, I was passing
> judgment on them ... especially the elder brother.... My names for
> them were really labels and to label a person is sometimes to be done
> with that person. Labels easily become walls. Aren't labels boxes into
> which we put people? ... By trying to label the prodigal and the
> elder brother I discovered I was saying something about my likes and
> dislikes in people, and probably what I like and dislike about myself.
> [P]

In leading us through an examination of his thought process about
the two brothers—which, not incidentally, turns out to be more about
the speaker himself than about the objects of his thinking—the pastor
suggests that one should not be premature in passing judgment on the
brothers. But as the excerpt progresses, we see the stronger problem
here—the speaker's self-doubt that he can be justified in evaluating the
boys at all. It is not simply that the pastor feels the need to examine all
sides of the story, or get inside the heads of the brothers, or provide
accounts for them that diminish the idea of blame. It is that he is questioning the very existence of legitimate grounds for authoritative moral
and theological knowledge. When one speaks theologically, the sermon asks, is it possible to know whether one is presenting truths or
merely speaking about one's own subjectivity, about one's own personal preferences? If one cannot be reasonably sure one is speaking the
truth, how is it possible to judge? In other words, the pastor poses an
essential challenge to the possibility of objective theological speech, by
asking: Isn't all talk—even religious talk, even from an allegedly authoritative speaker—merely about the self? We might wonder whether
such penetrating self-doubts do not at least partially inform weak Presbyterian notions of sin in general and, specifically, the articulation of
tolerance that marks the other sermons in this set.

Conclusions

"Sin is not such a popular word," says one Southern Baptist preacher. "It may be out of our lexicons," he continues, "but it certainly isn't out of our lives." Given the voluntarist, self-assertive, and pragmatic orientation of contemporary American culture, we may even be somewhat surprised at the frequency with which "sin" appears in the vocabulary of our speakers, marked as a topic of concern. On the surface, it might seem that the very presence of talk about sin itself is an important form of resistance against our wider cultural constructions. We may be tempted to conclude that as the pastors measure the conduct of human beings against the claims that God makes on their lives, as they set up God's will and desires as the grounding for self-assessment and the direction of faith and conduct, and as they constitute disobedience to God's word as the ultimate transgression, they are providing a sharp alternative to our popular cultural notions that measure human conduct by yardsticks of practical rationality, of mundane success, and of the end-products of feelings of security and gratification.

Yet, as we have seen here, a closer examination of the sermons suggests the many ways in which the concept of "sin" has been accommodated to fit secular sensibilities. For while some traditional images of sin are retained in this speech, the language frequently cushions the listener from their impact, as it employs a variety of softening rhetorical devices. We have looked in depth at these rhetorical strategies: the device of depersonalization, which renders notions of sinfulness vague and abstract; the device of selectivity, exemplified in the omission of the foundational doctrine of original sin; the device of deflection, through which sin is projected off listeners and onto groups of outsiders; the device of mitigation, employed to modify the potential for audience identification with sinful characters; and the device of therapeutic tolerance, through which sin is translated as errant behavior, explanations for misdeeds are sought in the social context rather than in the individual, and the response of judgment is replaced by that of empathy. In its most extreme formulation, we have seen how the application of therapeutic tolerance to the idea of sin quashes even the possibility of authoritative religious speech, rendering the speaker silent on any matter except for the musings of his own subjectivity.

Yet, in many of the sermons, judgment against sin is in fact rendered—though not aimed at the speakers' listeners—and its precise formulations and the nature of its targets may give us some pause. We may see reason to reconsider the notion of civility which some scholars have used to describe certain tendencies of contemporary religious speech. In their definitions, civility softens speech into politeness and inoffensiveness, and is marked by acceptance, or at least tolerance, of the beliefs of others. In these sermons, at least, speech is polite, but certainly not universally tolerant of cultural and religious differences. While "insiders" are cushioned from the potential for offense, "outsiders"—here constituted as children, the social underclass, and Jews— are fair game for chastisement and censure. These findings might suggest that while care is taken not to appear unattractive to actual or potential members of the congregation, civility does not necessary extend into norms of tolerance for those outside the reach of the church. Indeed, specifically with respect to speech about Jews, we might wonder whether the very politeness of the speech allows speakers in the modern context to insinuate ancient stereotypes that it might seem less legitimate for them to discuss directly. In this context, talk about sin appears more to be setting implicit boundaries to separate insiders who are beyond the reach of evaluation from outsiders who are targets for it than to be articulating theological insights into the depravity of human nature.

CHAPTER SIX

The Transformed Self

And he arose and came to his father. But while he was yet at a
   distance, his father saw him and had compassion, and ran and
   embraced him and kissed him.
And the son said to him, "Father, I have sinned against heaven
   and before you. I am no longer worthy to be called your son."
But the father said to his servants, "Bring quickly the best
   robe, and put it on him; and put a ring on his hand, and shoes
   on his feet;
and bring the fatted calf and kill it, and let us eat and make
   merry; for this my son was dead, and is alive again; he was
   lost, and is found."
   (*Luke 15:20–24, Revised Standard Version*)

Aɴᴅ sᴏ ᴛʜᴇ prodigal son reaches the end of his journey. Luke tells
us that as the young man comes to himself, he lifts himself out of the
pigpen, guided by memories of the comforts and security of his father's
house, and returns home. There he is greeted by his father, who grants
unconditional forgiveness and acceptance symbolized by the gift of the
sandals, robe, and ring, and by the rejoicing at the feast. Although the
account Luke gives is only a few sentences long, many of the pastors
linger in their sermons on the scene of the son's homecoming, as they
demonstrate its application to their listeners. For the return of the prodigal son represents the event of conversion in the life of the individual.
It is the moment when, confronted with God's inexplicable and unde-
served grace, the configuration of the self is changed. Through conversion, a person undergoes a break between the old self that lives in the
world before the transmutative experience and a different self that is
brought into being through the salvific relationship with Jesus Christ.

Tʜᴇᴏʟᴏɢɪᴄᴀʟ Lᴀɴɢᴜᴀɢᴇs ᴏꜰ Tʀᴀɴsꜰᴏʀᴍᴀᴛɪᴏɴ

The language used above suggests that of Paul and Augustine, who
provide a vocabulary on which pastors could draw in talking about the
transformation of the self. In this speech, the replacement of the old self

by the new is a grace-infused shedding of sin, a ridding of mortal nature tuned into gratification of desires that inevitably lead to death. The
demise of the "old man" requires the removal of self-centeredness, of
love for the self and for control over the things of the world—all of
which blind human beings to the nature of their true love, that of God.
The change can be effected, however, only through God's grace. Even
though human beings may know the good, their inner selves are so
perverted that they are incapable of choosing it. Only as God trans-
forms the will through the saving act can the self be redirected toward
the good God desires and turn men and women away from their sinful
nature.[1]

This Augustinian vocabulary prevailed in Calvinist speech throughout the early years of American Protestantism. Soon after the First
Great Awakening, however, the harshness of the doctrine underwent
modification that continues to the present day. This modification in-
jected other vocabularies into speech about the self, which have given
voice to different conceptions of human nature and human agency.

One such change, with far-reaching implications for religious
speech, reversed the way in which the notion of the self is discussed.
Both the Puritans and major schools of thinkers during the First Great
Awakening described the self mainly through negative attributes, seeing concern with the self as an inducement to sin. Self-love was concep-
tualized as selfish will, which turns unregenerate people toward
earthly desires and constitutes an impenetrable barrier to conversion.[2]

But by the middle of the eighteenth century, as a result of the influence of developments in British and Scottish philosophy, the notion
began to catch on that self-love can, in fact, be instrumental in human
regeneration. The sentiment of self-love (self-esteem, self-enjoyment)
came to be viewed as a beneficial instinct which God had instilled in
human beings for the purpose of calling them to repentance.[3] It is
through self-love, these theologies taught, that human beings are re-
called to that which is benevolent and good in their God-given nature.

This period also saw emphasis on the role of the individual's feelings
in both religious conversion and the Christian life. The Second Great
Awakening gave birth to a host of devotional societies—Bible classes,
prayer meetings, and benevolent groups—in which believers were en-
couraged to air their opinions and disclose their feelings about spiritual
matters. The religious role of sentiment was also bolstered by the
development of regional tract societies, which became unified and formalized as the American Tract Society around 1825. The group pub-

lished and circulated millions of pamphlets containing emotional appeals to the unconverted in language frequently laced with sentimentality.[4] These appeals were not meant to supplant, only to supplement, traditional rationalistic accounts of Christianity, but their emphasis on the affect of the individual helped pave the way for subsequent changes in American Protestant ideas of the self.

By the end of the nineteenth century, liberal theologians were contributing a new set of images around the self and the process of internal change. Consonant with liberalism's optimistic view of human nature and capabilities, and its belief in the unity and harmony of nature, these thinkers reconfigured the process of conversion. In their view, one comes to the conversion experience through trust in one's inner religious voice, a voice through which an immanent God provides promptings toward change.[5] The key to salvation thus lies within the self; the charge to the individual person is to listen and be receptive to this inner voice.[6] Also, since sin was regarded largely as error or ignorance (consonant with liberal beliefs in the essential goodness of humankind), the view prevailed that behavioral change can come about through education about ethical and moral concerns.[7]

Popularization of ideas taken from the burgeoning science of psychology early in the twentieth century left deep and lasting marks on conceptions of the self. At the start of the movement, liberal theologians and practitioners were drawing on popular psychological ideas about the problems of the self as a sense of unhappiness and powerlessness caused by a lack of "adjustment" to the social and natural environments. Translating these concepts into their own terms, religious speakers discussed faith in God as a kind of therapy that would help men and women deal with the demands of the real world.[8] Neo-orthodox theologians later criticized this stance, not only for its view of religious faith as a means to a secular end, but also for its acceptance of the legitimacy of prevailing social values and institutions.[9] Both criticisms were to leave their mark—although to different extent—on the psychologically influenced ideas of the self prevalent in liberal Protestant speech since the Second World War.

Spearheaded by the humanistic psychology of Carl Rogers, which emerged in the context of social and psychotherapeutic critiques of mass culture, a major current of postwar pastoral psychology reconceived the problem of selfhood as a lack of "self-realization." In this view, men and women are enjoined to recover an authentic self, a self of freedom, moral goodness, and interpersonal sensitivity, from the constraints of binding social institutions. The pastoral counseling session is the paradigmatic experience through which a person can achieve self-realization. As the pastor-therapist adopts a nonjudgmental stance of empathy with the client's self-disclosures, the client is freed to discover and express emotions without constraint.[10] Realization of the potential of the self results from acceptance of the self—first, as it is modeled for the client by the therapist, and eventually as the client learns to accept his own being. While contemporary Protestant theologians argue about the extent to which psychotherapeutic concepts and models are useful in spiritual growth, some theologians are attempting to find a synthesis between certain traditional Christian notions (for example, sin) and humanistic psychological thinking about the role of self-acceptance in personal development.[11]

From the notion of perverse sin-nature to the call for self-acceptance, American Protestant theology has provided adherents with diverse vocabularies for speaking of the self. What do the sermons tell us about contemporary formulations in the two denominations?

CONVERSION AS SELF-FULFILLMENT

In the following sections, I examine the sermons' teachings about the self as they tell a tale about transformation through conversion. For the most part, these narratives are present in Southern Baptist, rather than Presbyterian, sermons (they appear in 85 percent of the Southern Baptist sermons), most likely because Presbyterians practice infant baptism. Nevertheless, a handful of the Presbyterian sermons studied here (12 percent) include talk about conversion as they interpret the behavior of the prodigal son in returning home. In both groups, we shall note the enormous influence of modern secular psychology on the speech as the traditional notion of conversion—the act of turning one's love from sin to God—is frequently reconstituted as the realization of personal fulfillment. In many of the sermons, the impetus to convert lies not so much in the need to grapple with sin-nature or the desire to avoid eternal punishment as in the promise of two rewards highly valued in popular psychology: the satisfaction of discovering one's true, authentic self; and the fulfillment that comes through realization of a "meaningful, intimate relationship" with another. We shall see how this speech guides listeners to an exploration of their deepest selves, how it depicts a longing on the part of each person for the fulfillment of a meaningful relationship, and how it promises immediate satisfaction of that need through the event of conversion (frequently constituted as an act of emotional bonding with God).

As they urge their listener to undergo the experience of conversion, the speakers first probe the depths of the individual's interior self. Despite the complexities of the self, the language is often constructed here so as to make the conversion event as easy as possible to achieve. All the qualities necessary to attain a "meaningful, intimate relationship"—emotional self-awareness, openness, and receptivity—are depicted as innate in human nature. There is no need in the speech of the sermons for the individual to struggle with sin-nature or a recalcitrant will, since the psychological raw materials from which the post-conversion self is forged are already present and are easily brought to the fore where they await God's refining procedures. Thus, for some speakers, the event of conversion depends on a fluid, spontaneous "movement of the heart," which heightens the sense of the free availability and efficacy of conversion once desire is acknowledged.

But the innate qualities that serve the individual's ability to incorporate God into the heart could also, of course, be used to achieve alternative "meaningful relationships": with other individual human beings, with the human community. Thus, the sermons work to motivate conversion as the *sole* means of achieving a fulfilling, intimate relationship. Not only does the speech of the sermons depict God as a uniquely fitting interpersonal partner for humankind, it also debunks the possibility of trustworthy human intimacy. As the nature and need of the individual are constituted in this speech, no road except conversion is left open.

The presentation in this chapter differs from that given to other issues in this book because the topic of conversion is treated relatively homogeneously by a relatively small group of speakers. Instead of describing the range of discourses, a composite account is presented that represents general tendencies.[12]

I begin looking at the sermons' talk about the essential self: the moral and psychological qualities said to constitute human nature.

FREE WILL AND HUMAN NATURE

A pastor opens his sermon with this little story:

A father [went] with his little son to tuck him in for the night. They kneeled together beside the bed to pray. The little boy began to pray asking God to bless his cat, dog, gold fish, and sister and mommy and daddy. He then paused for a moment and began to pray the Lord's Prayer, saying, "Our Father who art in heaven, how do you know my name?" Now we do not know if the little boy was overwhelmed by the word "Hallowed" and therefore misunderstood it, or whether he was making an honest inquiry to God about his own personhood. But I believe you would agree with me he was asking a very important question of God. [SB]

The sermon goes on to suggest that God knows every person's name because he is a daddy, who cares for humankind as individuated persons just as a human daddy knows and loves his own children. But there is another issue at play here, one addressed by most of the sermons. The pastor uses the question raised in the boy's misspeaking of the prayer to ask not only how God knows and loves each person, but also how people reach an understanding of their own identities. Instead of positing a unique and separate personality, the answer given here grounds the complexities of the self in a fundamental basis. Although each person's relationship with God is private and individual, yet all people share an essential human nature, given by God and capable of being described in terms of universal characteristics.

For these pastors, the notion of human nature is inextricably linked to God's agency in creation. God made men and women as he would, and their qualities have no source other than God's volition. Among other things, what God wishes for human beings is their free will, the capacity to make their own choices. The importance of qualities of autonomy and dignity is heightened precisely because they indicate God's love for humankind. People were created free because to do otherwise would be to insult them, to make their intelligence superfluous, to mar their essential selves.

One speaker makes the analogy between the behavior of the prodigal son and all of human nature:

Just as God does with us, [the father of the prodigal son] did not violate his son's personality by refusing [to let him go]. You are free to make choices contrary to God's will, but God holds you responsible for your choices. . . . This responsibility combines the dignity and the danger of decision. The father loves us. He will not force his will on us. [SB]

Another pastor suggests that the doctrine of free will demonstrates the regard God has for his human creatures. Not only does God love them, he respects their intelligence, ability, and autonomy. Although God could have created human beings otherwise, he has made them free to chart the course of their own lives:

> What kind of God, after all, would so manipulate his intelligent creatures that they either have no mind to choose, or nothing between which to choose? In great love, God has set us free to become and to be, to take charge and be responsible for our own destinies. [SB]

As another pastor emblematically phrases it:

> God made us sons, not slaves. [SB]

It follows that the free will characterizing human nature extends to the decision to sin. Just as human beings may decide to walk in the path of righteousness and obedience, so they may freely choose to walk away, to rebel against God. A pastor says:

> We have a choice in life. One son chose to leave home; the other stayed: the choice was theirs. You see, being created in the image of God means for one thing that we have a will to choose. Mankind was elevated above the other creation, but with our choices comes the responsibility. [SB]

Another adds:

> A lot of us, all of us, have at one time or another been in that far country. We choose to go there, you know. No one sends us there. [SB]

Free will also leaves human beings at liberty to reject God's promise of forgiveness. Even when they hear him calling, people may choose to block their ears. The same speaker continues, using a formulation that parallels Augustine's famous attempt to bargain with God for time over his need for chastity:

> We hear the voice of God. We are in a far country, miserable, unhappy, and we want to come back to God, but we just put God off. . . . We say, "God, I know you want me back, but listen, Lord, I'll come back, but give me a few more moments. Give me a little more time. Maybe I can pull myself up by my own bootstraps." [SB]

Left like this, the doctrine of free will sounds existentially bleak. If God simply has left people free, on what basis do they make decisions about faith or appropriate conduct? The answer is supplied by further construction of human nature, as the pastors depict the other essential qualities.

INNATE HUMAN GOODNESS

We have already seen some speakers articulate the doctrine of the universal sinfulness of human beings. Just as this potentially distasteful concept is palliated, in talk about sin, by being transferred onto other people, so its force is softened in talk about human nature. For the speakers who explicitly address this issue, human nature is either presented as thoroughly good or an unbalanced admixture of good and bad, with good prevailing. This language draws on the undoing of the doctrine of human depravity and the salience of the Fall, which began in the Second Great Awakening in America. Without saying so, and without marking the contrast between human beings' God-given goodness and the departure from it in Adam and Eve's sin, the speech emphasizes people's pristine state of original goodness. As one speaker preaches:

> God doesn't make junk in the first place. [SB]

Another pastor describes the goodness of human nature through its likeness to God, an identity known to every human being, no matter how obliquely:

> The Colossian hymn [says], "You know you were created in the image of God." You were. And that image is the image of Jesus Christ. You were created through him and for him. He is the secret about who you are. He is the clue to your own true self. [SB]

Similarly, another pastor describes the innate goodness of human beings and the drive it supplies for connection with God:

> When Jesus says that [the prodigal son] came to himself, He pays us the highest of compliments, for He suggests that there is something within the human being which innately wants goodness and love, which wants to be at home and in harmony with the will of God. [P]

For some speakers, the innate goodness of humankind presents itself as interior knowledge, instinctive awareness of the God-given moral standards by which human beings should judge their own behavior. Note that, in the following excerpt, when concession is made to the doctrine of humankind's sinful nature, the concession is qualified ("*sometimes* that sense it distorted"):

There is a desire for righteousness in you. There is a hunger for purity. Deep down inside you believe in justice, honesty, and faithfulness. The standards of God are a part of our own make-up. We were created in the image of God no matter how marred that image. We do have a sense of right and wrong. Sometimes that sense is distorted, but deep down, a man's sense of right and wrong seems to correspond to what God has said. [SB]

Another sermon furthers the imagery of inborn moral awareness by citing a piece of moralizing doggerel from which I draw the excerpt below. Human beings may, and indeed must, monitor and evaluate their own behavior precisely because they possess an internal gauge of goodness. Note the emphasis on purely internal standards, which underscores attributes of autonomy and individualization frequently pronounced in Southern Baptist speech. These standards are not idiosyncratic, however, since they are "hard-wired" into human beings through God's act of creation. Thus, in the verse, the "guy in the glass" functions as a God-given superego for each person to put a check on unbridled behaviors:

When you get what you want in your struggle for wealth and the world makes you king for a day,
Then go to the mirror and look at yourself and see what that guy (or gal) has to say.
For it isn't your father or mother or wife who judgment upon you must pass,
The fellow who's verdict counts most in your life is the guy staring back from the glass. . . . [SB]

The Psychology of Openness

If the self is both intrinsically moral and aware of its moral nature, it is characterized even more explicitly by a second set of characteristics and abilities, a set that forms the core of personhood around which conversion can work. As human beings are portrayed in this speech, they innately long to reach out for a relationship with another that is intimate, fulfilling, and interdependent. People are also seen as innately possessing the qualities necessary to achieve such a relationship, as it is presented by contemporary popular psychology. In order to reach out and construct "meaningful relationships" with others, popular psychology teaches, one must be able to express one's deepest feelings and be responsive to the expressed feelings of one's partner.[13] Thus, too, many of the sermons present human nature in terms of its fundamental qualities of openness and receptivity: the desire and ability to communicate the most intimate needs of the self, honestly and without reserve, both to the self and to another; and the ability to relate sensitively and empathically to the interpersonal partner (who is meant in this speech, of course, to be God).

TRUST AND SELF-DISCLOSURE

The sermons teach that innate within the human self is the impulse toward openness, the drive and ability to know oneself fully and to make that self deeply available to a chosen partner. Self-knowledge and self-disclosure are essential for an intimate relationship, these sermons suggest, even though self-disclosure places people at risk of embarrassment and attributions of weakness. In order to take the risk, one must trust the conversational partner to whom intimate details are revealed. But, the sermons argue, trust is also an innate human quality, a characteristic of the primal interior self, although people's experience in the world may teach them to resist its promptings.

Speakers reach to a model of those in a "natural state" (variously depicted as before society or before sin) to furnish examples of the innate openness and trust of humankind. The story of the praying boy, quoted above, best captures this idea: the innocent child transforming the ritual recitation of the Lord's Prayer into an unselfconscious and personalized query to God. He simultaneously poses a question to the Almighty of private concern and freely reveals his anxiety over such a basic issue as self-identity ("how do you know my name?"). One lesson underscored here is that this is precisely how one *will* feel free to talk with God once conversion has done its work, as the quality of intimate self-disclosure, harking back to the innocent state of childhood honesty, is portrayed as part of a correct relationship with the divine. As a preacher says:

> I can come to God and I can say dear Lord, I've got myself in this mess, this problem, this trouble, and I don't know how to get out. Would you give me some wisdom so I know how to get out of this? [SB]

Openness is not only the original tendency of humankind in relationships with significant others, it is presented here as the *natural* tendency, "hard-coded" into human associations based on biological necessity. In the following excerpt, a pastor portrays the state of openness that characterizes the relationship between infant and parent. Openness is linked not only to feelings of trust and intimacy, but to obedience as well:

> We begin our human pilgrimage utterly united to our mothers—we are part and parcel of their very bodies and even after the trauma of birth itself a sense of trust and openness persists. We essentially idolize our parents and we follow their teachings and directions. We are willing to do whatever they say. [SB]

Indeed, the openness of self-revelation, of trust and the obedience that follows it, are so nearly primal that here they are made constitutive of humankind's original experience: Adam and Eve's relationship with God in Paradise. As a pastor says:

> [In using the word "abba" to address God,] Jesus was seeking to bring us back to our Adam and Eve experience with God as Father of the Garden, as we trust him in faith again. [SB]

The metaphor of the Garden evokes linkages between openness and humankind's God-given natural state. Not only does the metaphor call forth images of man and woman unselfconsciously revealed to each other and to God in a world before sin, it recalls another way in which human beings' original relationship with God was open and unencumbered: that it was completely unmediated, as man and God spoke face-to-face. No artificial barriers stood in the way of the essential connection.

Memories of the Garden are embedded within the consciousness of every human being, one pastor preaches. In the next excerpt, the metaphor of the Garden serves both to underscore the human quality of openness and to pave the way for speech about profound feelings of longing to recapture the primal connection with God. Longing is evoked both through the journey of memory and through the use of a poetic form of talk:

> The Bible tells us that home-sickness is the plight of all of us born of heaven's spark, cast from a garden, settling east of Eden, living in a world of suspicion and sin. So the poet, Henry Vaughan, wrote of Adam's fall:
>
>> He drew the Curse upon the world, and Crackt
>> The whole frame with his fall.

> This made him long for home, as loathe to stay
> With murmurers, and foes;
> He sigh'd for Eden, and would often say
> Ah! what bright days were those.

With Adam and Eve, we sigh for Eden, we long for home, we yearn wistfully for a time buried deep in our past, in the past of the world, in the past of time and space and eternity when we were at home. [SB]

It is precisely one's feelings that are necessary to recover the childhood of the world, the childhood of the self—the revelation of self-awareness, the knowledge of who one really is. Here, in imagery present in much of the sermons' speech about openness and receptivity, people are taught the appropriate techniques for working on their innate resources in order to heighten their effectiveness. As a pastor says:

> There's a school of psychology, as you know, that is saying that all of us are out of touch to some extent. . . . Gestalt therapy is saying things like this: "Sit still for a moment. . . . Are you angry inside? Do you feel joy about life, or sadness? Is there peace in you, or turmoil?" [P]

For some speakers, it is the Gestalt-like moment experienced by the prodigal son in the pigpen that brings him to self-awareness. The son gets back "in touch" with his true identity as the inner voice of feelings opens up and reveals himself to himself. As one preacher teaches:

> It was in the loneliness and the quiet of the barnyard as I imagine perhaps at midnight, no longer any phony friends around him, no noise or confusion. The text says, "He came to himself." He had not been himself until then. He was not at peace, not integrated, not together, as we say. [P]

This formulation appears in another sermon, highlighting the emphatic, urgent nature of the message that the self sends the self:

> Jesus says, "Finally he got in touch with himself. . . . "He cried aloud," the narrative says. At last, coming to his senses, he cried aloud. *He heard himself.* He couldn't deny it, he couldn't turn away from it, because he heard the cry. It came out, loud and clear. (emphasis in original) [P]

ACCRETIONS AND AUTHENTICITY

As these excerpts show, human nature provides both the raw materials and the drive for conversion. But people are not automatically "in touch" with their true identity. The authentic self of goodness, created in God's image, is invariably overlain with other characteristics during the human sojourn in the world. The goal self-awareness is said to serve—one's ultimate reunification with God—cannot be achieved until people understand that the authentic self is covered with layers of artifice that prevent them from reaching God. Here, the work of feelings does not suffice. The sermons call on each person to study the self, to learn about the effects of daily life on the core of human nature. Once the self is understood in this way, the sermons teach, human beings will acknowledge their wish to overthrow the accumulation of false characteristics and stand before God, readied for the event of conversion.

For a few speakers, who retain formulations that suggest those of some early church fathers, the artificial accretions that cling to the self are the result of sin.[14] In the following excerpt, sin covers the soul as scar tissue covers a wound. Human beings cannot recognize the essential worthiness of their nature because the sins of their lives hide that light from them:

> Maybe we say, "God, I'm so unworthy [to come to you]. I'm too unworthy to be your son. I've been scarred from the sins of my life. I've spent my life in its poisonous ghettoes. I'm not worthy to be called your son." [SB]

Similarly, another speaker describes sin as a set of attitudes that act as a mesh cover might on a jar, allowing access to the superficial layers but suppressing the pure material in the hidden core:

> The Old Testament had three words for sin: rebellion; missing the mark; and iniquity or overstepping the law. We must face the truth. These [words describe] certain attitudes which keep us from coming home, which hide us from our own true selves. They keep God's image in us buried deeply within us. [SB]

The next excerpt furthers the imagery of sin as fetter and suppression. Here the speech concerns ways in which the spark of the inner self, once it begins its process of self-realization, struggles to free itself from the suffocating enclosure woven out of the strands of sin:

We've all been there, trapped in our sins with no way out and no hope. Suddenly we hear the voice of God and what a ray of sunshine that is. Here in this very room, people who are caught and fettered in their sins, suddenly God's grace comes into their lives and they become new creatures, reconciled to God. [SB]

For other speakers, the accretion that obscures the self stems, instead, from the social practices of the secular world as they affect one's biography. In this speech, the characteristics of personality that people acquire in the course of life accumulate on top of the essential self. They are cleverly disguised, because they are socially and personally validated as real, but they are sham, nevertheless. Thus one pastor describes the self, encrusted with layers of stuff that it has picked up during its sojourn in the world, in terms of an artifact—a soda bottle—that he has dug up from a nearby riverbank. Just as the inert bottle has accumulated a crust of coral that does not naturally belong to it, so the self, in a life course without God, is surrounded by artificial overlays. Not only is the enshelled self inauthentic, prevented from being what it essentially is, but it is also out of place, disordered, and lost. Therefore it cannot serve its rightful purpose. The self is bound, not only from authenticity and usefulness to one's own true self, but from others as well:

This is a bottle. In fact, it's a 7-Up bottle. But it's a bottle that's encrusted with coral. Coral is the remains of dead sea creatures. There's fisherman's line hung on it. It's probably yours. And the fish that you caught is a piece of coral now. That's what happens to us when we get lost and out of place. Where no one can receive the benefits of our true selves. We get covered up. Dead. And we become a snag and a hindrance. [SB]

Another speaker attributes the accretion surrounding the true self to the effects of society. In this excerpt, the authentic self is at the center of a circle, englobed and partially disguised by the reified influences of society and secular culture, agents of socialization, and one's autobiography. Yet note here, as in the previous excerpt, that the layers of artifice do not invade the central self. The core of authenticity at the heart of the circle remains inviolate, although it may be hidden from view:

Picture your own true self at the center of a circle. Around that center are many layers that shape the self, some good, some not so good; layers of cultural and social conditioning, layers of parental formation and nurture, and experiences, good and bad. All these things have the capacity to hide from you your own true self. [SB]

For some Presbyterian speakers, the accretion that surrounds the true self results from dysfunctional patterns of individual behavior: unquestioned habits that rigidify thinking, illusions about life's realities, failure to monitor one's activities to see whether one is in touch with the real world. These accretions can be seen as "defenses" that people erect against their recognition of their authentic selves. In the next excerpt, which we have already seen in another context, the process by which the prodigal son "comes to himself" is described, as he realizes the nature of the barriers to his true self that emprison him in the inappropriateness and unhappiness of inauthenticity:

It was in the loneliness and quiet of the barnyard as I imagine perhaps at midnight, no longer any phony friends around him, no noise of confusion. The text says, "He came to himself." . . . There somehow he realized that he was not free but enslaved, enslaved to his own urges, enslaved to his illusions and his habits. [P]

Another Presbyterian joins these themes in a discussion of the "reality check" Jesus provides as the self endeavors to throw off its accumulated layers of falsehood. Here, Jesus functions as a divine therapist, bringing his human conversational partner to a state of being in touch with the truths of human nature and human needs:

I love Jesus because he brings us to the point we need to be. He understands what it is to be human . . . to "come to our senses" and recognize what life really is for us now, and stop constructing. [P]

Human Beings as God's Children

Thus far, the speech of these sermons has identified a fundamental human nature at the core of every person: innately good, open to self-understanding, and in need of release from the artifice hiding its true identity. But it is easy to see how these formulations, taken alone, could pose problems for religious speakers. Framed as they are in the language of humanistic psychology, they could be understood to suggest secular alternatives to the religious solution of conversion. For nothing in this speech so far suggests that a person cannot reach fulfillment through purely secular means. How do the pastors suggest that these potential alternatives cannot be sufficient? How do they warrant the act of reaching out to God as the sole means by which to find and realize the self?

The speakers' solution is that the process of self-awareness is never depicted as a voyage forward but always as a journey back—a process of recollection whereby one "remembers" the origin of the self. The realization of identity is linked to the notion of its grounding in an essential relationship with God—no matter how far from the experience of that relationship one may have strayed.[15] What one discovers in the exploration of the self is its bond to its author. As that bond is recognized, the speech creates a powerful evocation of longing to re-enact and restore the terms of the fundamental relationship of connection and meaning. Without this relationship, one speaker preaches, there is no authentic self-knowledge, since there cannot be an authentic self:

> To come home to your own true self is to come home to God. To come home to God is to come to your own true self. Let me put it Christologically. When you look at Jesus Christ you see at the same time God's face and your own true face. When you follow him and receive his love you come home both to God and to your own true self. [SB]

A person's identity is in fact defined by his role as a child of God, another pastor preaches, a role which pre-exists the individual person and which can never be abrogated no matter what one's behavior:

> [God] reaches out and grabs hold of us and says, "You are my son, you've always been my son. Your name is my name, you can never lose that. You will always be a part of this family." [SB]

Thus, a pastor suggests, there is a more compelling reason for "getting in touch with one's feelings" than mere self-awareness, as the practice of monitoring the self leads to an understanding of God:

> Is it possible that if we followed our feelings, got in touch with where we really are, it would lead us to God? That shouldn't be too surprising, since He created us in His image, and our creation is meant to be in touch with Him. So if we got in touch with our true feelings, we'd be on the road to getting in touch with Him. [P]

But embarking on the road to God requires more instruction about one's inner qualities, as the open and emotionally resonant person learns to reach out beyond the self to make the connection with God.

Here the sermons elaborate on another psychological characteristic with which the interior self has been invested: one's resources of receptivity, which allow the self to listen empathically to the messages of the would-be partner.

REACHING OUT TO GOD

Just as the voice of the feelings opens the self to the self, communicating the awareness of self-identity, so the sensitivities of the self are honed so that it can now "hear" the voice of God, the conversational partner. His constant messages become clearly heard once one is attuned to his voice. One pastor preaches:

> Sometimes when we put God off we discover that our hearing is not as good because over a period of time slowly the voice of God fades away. It's not that God has quit calling. It's simply that we've quit listening, and we become insensitive to him and we no longer hear his voice. [SB]

Thus, the solution to the diminished capacity to hear is given:

> Trust God. If you trust God you become vulnerable and open and his voice becomes louder in your heart and you hear him over and over again. . . . As we allow our hearts to be open, God comes into them. [SB]

Once the heart is opened, God's voice is ubiquitous, available when people most need to hear it. As this excerpt puts it:

> Hear it today—God's music coming across the field, through the street or down the hallway—or into your late night struggles with your own worth. Let it be for you the music of reunion, the glad music of God's love for you. [P]

As these excerpts suggest, learning to listen to God is well worth the effort, for it is self-reinforcing and full of rewards. The content of God's communication is overwhelmingly supportive. As one pastor preaches, once the interior self is opened up to receive God's voice, it tunes into a message of complete affirmation:

> At the deepest level of your being . . . you are utterly loved, fully received, unconditionally accepted by God. . . . At that truest and deepest level, God comes to say, "John, Mary, I love you, you are my child, I will never stop loving you. Come home." [SB]

This, then, is the ideal self awaiting conversion: aware of its dignity and ability to make choices; stripped of artifice and "defenses;" open to the communication of its inner voice concerning its feelings; longing for the fulfillment of an intimate relationship; and primed to hear God's messages of love and support. What remains to be constructed through the preachers' speech is the necessity of receiving God into the heart as the *only* possible recourse to realizing true selfhood. Here, many of the sermons draw on images to hammer two points home: that the acceptance of conversion is the only appropriate response of the open and empathic self to God, since he wishes it so strongly and suffers its lack with every passing moment; and that there is no possible route to the fulfillment the essential self needs and seeks other than through God.

Empathy with God

Once the psychological buffers to receptivity have been removed, and people begin hearing God's reassuring messages of support and concern, they become attuned to another aspect of God's message: the divine voice calling out in longing and need for reunion with humankind. In chapter three I described ways in which many of the sermons characterize God in terms of *his* emotional needs. The function of these characterizations becomes clear now in the context of talk about conversion, as the speech constructs a powerful appeal to accepting salvation based on one's emotional identification with God's feelings. Heightened sensitivity to one's own emotional need leads seamlessly to the notion of empathy with God. In these appeals, one is driven to conversion, not only for one's own, but also for *God's* sake—to spare him further fruitless efforts, to spare him hurt and disappointment. Just as the psychology of openness that characterizes human beings leads them to become aware of their needs and to reveal them, so God is driven to open himself up to his feelings, to suffer on behalf of humankind and make his anguish known. And, given one's resources of empathy, it becomes one's duty to act to assuage God's suffering in the only way commensurate with the extent of his pain: by accepting the emotional connection of conversion.

We have already observed the tendency in many of the sermons to simplify or mellow God's qualities so that the distance between humankind and God is abridged, and so that God may be readily understood. In part, this occurs as speakers discuss God's inner states—and particularly his feelings—in human terms. Here, God's emotions are made accessible to empathy as the pastors dwell on his feelings of parental pain, a result of the sacrifice of his son. Recall this excerpt in which a Southern Baptist speaker positions his listeners to empathize with God's feelings over the loss of his son, as one wears his shoes and undergoes his pain:

> Imagine for a moment how God must have felt seeing his Son leave home, knowing that he must be executed like a criminal for you and me. Jesus was God's favorite and only son. How would you like to see your son leave home knowing that this would happen to him? [SB]

Identification with God's feelings serves to motivate conversion in return for God's great sacrifice, as subsequent utterances in this sermon make clear:

> [God] has been patiently awaiting the day when you will come home to him. . . . Jesus had to die so that we could be forgiven for our sins. . . . You see, my friend, God demonstrates His love toward us in that while we were yet sinners, Jesus came to earth to pay for our sins. [SB]

Another pastor addresses the issue of God's suffering as a parent of wayward human beings. Note how the excerpt exploits qualities of openness and sensitivity as it makes the linkage, without argument or evidence, that to be a parent is to experience painful feelings:

> That's the way it is to be a parent. You make yourself vulnerable to pain. And that is the most amazing thing about God. Is that he voluntarily made himself susceptible to hurt and pain. And that's why I think it's so wrong of us to say, well my [continuing to] sin hurts nobody but me. Well it hurts God. He has a father's attitude. He loves you like a father. [SB]

Similarly, another pastor underscores God's painful feelings as he awaits the return of his wayward children. Note that this excerpt *assumes* that the appropriately empathic response of conversion will follow as one realizes the extent of God's suffering. People remain non-Christians not because of a desire to remain in sin, or because of membership in another faith community, but only because they do not understand the magnitude of God's agony of unfulfilled love:

> No one suffers more anguish over sinners than does God. . . . Perhaps you are a non-Christian. Maybe you have wondered just how God

feels about you. Maybe you didn't realize just how much God desires to love you if you would let him. [SB]

Further, some speakers suggest, once God's message of neediness has been received, it is impossible to tune it out, since God is persistent in his self-disclosure. One might as well comply at once with his desires, this excerpt implies, for God is not about to curtail his communication. This utterance turns the intensity of God's pain into an implied threat for the individual declining conversion:

> God won't be satisfied until you have salvation and He lives in your heart. . . . He won't ever quit looking. He will never give up on you. If you're running from God, rest assured that you will always have to run. He will forever be on your heels, searching to find you and bring you back. [SB]

Thus, another speaker suggests the persistence of God's search for his unsaved children:

> God's passion is single minded. He wants you home. He is like a shepherd searching as long as it takes, like a woman searching as long as it takes, like a father who waited as long as it took and then sprinted to welcome home his son. [SB]

THE INSUFFICIENCY OF HUMAN RELATIONSHIPS

The open, empathic self is not only receptive to God's communication of neediness, it is also defenseless against its own emotional pain. We have seen how the prior speech has portrayed human need as a longing for an intimate and fulfilling interpersonal relationship that requires self-disclosure based on trust of another. The speech represents the process by which the individual realizes the depth of internal emotional needs as he "gets in touch" with the inner self. But now, having created a need for that intimate connection, the sermons argue that trust in other human beings with respect to these needs is entirely misplaced. As they suggest, no one but God will fail to betray the exposed heart, the needy expression of the individual's deepest self. It is not only that God longs for the unique interpersonal relationship that he can supply for human beings, with which one should comply to spare God his misery. It is also that people, in their own need, have nowhere else to turn.[16]

As we might expect, pastors are most explicit in discussing this theme in preaching about the experiences of the prodigal son in the far country. I have already referred to the vivid elaborations Southern Baptist speakers tend to give of the younger brother's suffering in that alien place once he begins "to be in want," as the party ends and the famine strikes. In their talk about conversion, the sermons center on the failure of others to support the prodigal son when his sufferings begin. One pastor dramatizes the psychological pain of the needy son as he is betrayed by his colleagues:

> After a while famine comes in the far country. No longer is there a feast. Now there is loneliness, empty hearts, and thirsting souls, and we wish that someone would come and help us. [SB]

Another pastor emphasizes the plight of the prodigal son as his erstwhile friends desert him in his need. Note how he generalizes the situation of the biblical character to the contemporary world, in a formulation that continues the imagery we have already seen of the secular world as a pigpen:

> The far country looks like paradise to the young rebel when he enters it with time and health and money to burn. But when his resources are gone, the poor tramp discovers that his fair weather friends are gone too. We read that no man gave unto him. Where were all his buddies, the wild companions of his revelry? They always do a disappearing act when the famine sets in. The same liquor dealer that takes a man's money for the slop has no kind word or helping hand when the man has spent all. [SB]

Similarly, in the next excerpt, a person's trust in the comrades found in the world of pollution and sin is bound to be betrayed, despite the superficial attractions of forming these relationships. Other people are portrayed as unworthy of confidence and intimacy:

> If sin does anything, it drains us dry, and leaves us empty. Oh, it courts you, with all the grandeur and the glory that it promises, and it will walk with a multitude of people around you, wherever you go. . . . But when you become an alcoholic, when you spend all of your money, when you've become diseased, because of your involvement, when you become pregnant, because of your involvement, you suddenly find they aren't there anymore. . . . And the sad, sad tale that is always told of those who pursue that lifestyle is that ultimately some-

where you come to the moment when you are all alone. In need, and no one to care for your soul. [SB]

Not only is it the human being debased by sin who is vulnerable to the betrayal of trust by any partner other than God; as other excerpts suggest, every person, no matter what the behavior, ultimately is incapable of securing a relationship with another person that is self-disclosive, lasting, and dependable. For human relationships cannot possibly measure up to the unconditional acceptance, stability, and predictability of the intimate connection with God.

Commenting on the interpersonal styles of human beings, on the one hand, and God, on the other, this excerpt portrays wordly relationships as depersonalized, commodified, and interchangeable:

The world could care less what happens to you. You mess up your life, and they just get someone else to fill your place. You're expendable. You're not worth searching for. [SB]

In contrast:

God feels different about you. He loves you enough to search for you until he finds you. [SB]

Another preacher elaborates on the undependability of human relationships. Problems are caused by the tendency of people to evaluate one another, thus opening up the possibility of a withdrawal of love or approval. Note how the next excerpt *assumes* the tenets of Rogerian psychology, that what people need and want from those closest to them are relationships of unconditional acceptance:

If I discover some things about you, there's no way in the world I can ever think of you just like I once thought of you. I'm not saying that I would think of you in a condemnation kind of way, just that there is some knowledge there that I have of you that when I see you now, that's what I think of. That's why we are so closed about letting anything about our real selves come out. Because how many times have we sat down with somebody and we poured out our hearts and then later on we said, man I wish I hadn't said all that. [SB]

In contrast, God supplies a love undiminished by evaluation:

You see God is the only one who has the ability . . . to treat us as if we had never been away. . . . God treats me as if I'd never left home, treats me as if I'd never sinned. [SB]

Thus the sermons complete their tale of human nature and human need as they propel the individual toward conversion. There is only one more topic to cover, as the pastors give instructions on how the goal should be accomplished.

EFFECTIVE PROCEDURES

Up to this point, the preachers have been spinning a dramatic narrative about the journey of the self toward conversion. The narrative speeds along to its outcome. Driven to seek conversion, what more should the individual know and do? How does she bring herself—or ask to be transported—to the life-transforming event?

Here, the tone of the speech radically changes. The evocative language used to portray human nature and human need collapses into a technical appendix, into which preachers insert talk about the procedures of getting saved. The procedures are laid out like instructions in a recipe; they are prosaic, methodical, and direct.

The speech of the sermons falls into one of two categories, both of which, it appears, serve a similar end—to represent the process of conversion as organized and straightforward, contained by certain procedures whose correct implementation guarantees success. In the first formulation, procedures for conversion are standardized, presented as a methodical series of steps that order and rationalize one's activities. They codify conversion as a set of simple behavioral techniques that appear to lead systematically to the efficacious (and economical) achievement of the desired end; that suggest that there is one, and only one, legitimate path to the objective; and that call for compliance rather than reflection. Follow the formula, these sermons argue, and you are assured of reaching the goal. While the conversion appeals individuate listeners in that they are addressed to each solitary person, the instructions for procedures standardize the process, issuing the same set of directions for all.

Thus, the pastors itemize their instructions:

First you gotta admit your need. You gotta confess your sin, you've got to say, "Lord God everything your word says about me is true. And I need you, I need a savior." And then trust that savior: throw yourself on his mercy, call upon him to save you, and receive him and trust him with all your heart. [SB]

Similarly, another speaker lends the instructions clarity and memorability through the alliteration of their initial terms:

> Come back. How? Step by step we follow the story. The first step we call *recognition*. . . . We have to face up to ourselves, look honestly at ourselves and say, I have sinned. That's the first step in coming back. The next step is *realization* . . . you must accept yourself for what you are . . . say I recognize my limitations, I want something better but I have to start where I am. . . . Then [come] to the point of *responsibility* . . . this is very important in coming back . . . the prodigal son realized that, his life would never have changed if he had not faced the fact that he was responsible . . . and this leads to the next step, *restoration*: God loves us and has taken the initiative to provide the means of reconciliation and restoration. [SB]

The utterances in this first category depict conversion as necessitating human effort on a variety of fronts. The work of the intellect is required to realize one's status as a sinner. The work of the will is called into play in a potentially mortifying acknowledgment of human weakness. And the work of the affect is tapped to create the desire for reconciliation with God. All the major human faculties must collaborate before the desired end can be achieved. Because this is so, one gets the sense, if only indirectly, that there is room here for the experience of doubt and struggle, even for failure, as listeners are exhorted to place their entire selves on the line in the service of reaching the goal. Thus, for example, although intellect and affect may be positioned correctly, the will may lag behind. Indeed, some of the pastors leave an opening, in other contexts, for the possibility that conversion is not as easy as advertised.[17] One pastor comments thus on the prodigal son's delay in setting out for home:

> Much is often made of the son "coming to himself." No small wonder, alright. But the great wonder is that he waited so long. Why did he? Was it the powerful grip of the wayward life? Must he hit bottom before he could wake up? Was it his independent spirit? I submit that the reason he waited so long was because he knew something of his Father's great love. He knew that to go home broken and dirty, to look into his Father's eyes, to join in that happy family, would be just wonderful. But he also knew it would be HUMILIATING. (capitalized in original) [SB]

In contrast, the second type of formulation leaves no opening for doubt or failure; its speech presents the act of conversion as virtually foolproof. In these utterances, a person's work toward conversion is fully constituted by a "movement of the heart," an act of opening oneself to receiving God's messages of forgiveness and everlasting love and his partnership—all of which allow God to enter into one's affective experience. This talk is an achievement of economy and effectiveness. As the sermons have portrayed the stripping away of artifice and social convention (revealing the innate characteristics of openness, receptivity, and empathy), and as they have forged an emotional identification with God through their constitution of God's need, they have already *accomplished* the act of conversion for listeners by placing God inside their hearts. The speech is thus fully performative of the act. All that remains for the listener to do is simply acknowledge the work achieved in the prior talk.

As they instruct listeners on the procedures of conversion, little is left for the sermons to say. One preacher gives a typical formulation, a single sentence of directions:

> Open yourself to the salvation that God wants to work in your life. [SB]

As another speaker puts it, in only slightly more detail:

> If you would open your heart to God today, you would find Him as ready and willing to receive you as the father received the son in our story. [SB]

Thus pronounced, the instruction simplifies the process of conversion to its barest, and most readily achievable, state.

CONCLUSIONS

The course of the American Protestant experience has seen an increasing emphasis on the democratic and voluntarist nature of conversion, heightening the notion of the importance of individual self-knowledge and self-awareness in religious transformation. Once people become aware of themselves, this notion suggests, conversion is largely under their control.

The sermons analyzed in this chapter suggest an even greater emphasis on the idea of the readiness with which conversion takes place. Conversion is portrayed far less as the need to grapple with sin-nature than as a reorientation of one's psychology toward the creation of a close interpersonal relationship with God. In addition, human nature is constructed so as to invest it with all of the necessary psychological qualities for achieving the human being's part of the work of conversion. The talk serves to heighten certain characteristics that are innate in human beings and teaches listeners that they need to shed the artificial qualities that overshadow their essential selves. Once the inner self of the person is freed from artifice, she may achieve both the desire and the competence to form the interpersonal relationship with God. Satisfaction from human relationships is ruled out in this talk. The idea that God is suffering as he awaits a person's reunication with him forms the psychological motivations in this speech for the urge toward conversion. Once the personality is positioned in this way, the procedures of conversion are laid out as simple recipe steps that are easily achieved. Indeed, in one type of formulation, the work of conversion has already been performed for the individual as he comes to understand his nature. The risks of failure are minimized as technical procedures promise effective outcomes.

Secularity and Religious Speech

in the Two Denominations

Secularization presents Christianity with a nasty choice
between being relevant but undistinctive,
or distinctive but irrelevant.
(David Lyon, *The Steeple's Shadow*)

IN ATTEMPTING to understand the effects of modern secular culture on western religion, sociologists have investigated many aspects of religious faith and practice. Survey studies of such matters as the variables of religious growth and decline, church affiliation and attendance, and religious attitudes and beliefs have greatly enriched our knowledge about the state of religion in modern times. But these studies have neglected to consider the subtleties of the internal contents of religion—what some call its "meaning component." To be sure, surveys of religious opinion and faith have shed light on some aspects of religious ideology. But by their nature, these studies have been unable to probe the images, metaphors, and rhetorical formulations that inform belief and behavior. Although religious ideology, like all other ideologies, is created and maintained (or changed) through language, sociologists tend to overlook religious speech as a topic of research. As one sociologist of religion has observed: "Religious communities are awash in words . . . but about their discourse, we [know] virtually nothing."[1]

In response to this gap, this book has examined secularity in the Presbyterian Church (U.S.A.) and the Southern Baptist Convention through the perspective of language use, exploring the preaching of pastors as they explicate the Parable of the Prodigal Son. My goal has been to assess how this talk replies to conditions of modern secular culture. In the face of social processes of privatization, pluralization, and rationalization, I have asked, how do the churches respond? To what extent does the speech of contemporary Presbyterian and Southern Baptist sermons show adaptation to the contemporary secular culture? To what extent does it attempt to resist its force, or to reinterpret it through creative reformulations that reach beyond the opposing approaches?

To guide an examination of these issues, I have drawn on the work of contemporary theorists whose writings are amenable to viewing religion as a cultural system. Not only have they given us a better understanding of the social forces through which religion is impelled to confront secularity, they have also donated the useful categories of accommodation and resistance to describe certain strategies of response. I have systematized these speculations and drawn implications of these strategies for religious speech. In addition, I have tentatively added a third strategy, reframing, to name a potential style of response that, in keeping with contemporary understandings about the power of language, may use speech self-consciously to redefine the terms of the reply, neither denying the premises of secular culture nor surrendering to its demands.

We have seen how these strategies are used in the sermons to frame talk about theological and social issues, from images of God, to attitudes toward the world, doctrines of sin, and concepts of the self as it moves toward conversion. This study has allowed us not only to document the responses of the sermons in the context of secularity, but also to capture some of the complexity of the churches' speech as they attempt to work through the dilemmas of modernity for the expression of doctrines. The study gives fuller shape to theorists' categories as we see them put to use in the "practical art" of preaching.

I concluded each chapter of analysis by summarizing the styles of accommodating, resistant, and reframing discourses in the sermons' language. Now it is time to step back and assess the implications of this speech for religion in the secular context. Relevant but undistinctive? Distinctive but irrelevant? Or something else altogether?

THE DISCOURSE OF ACCOMMODATION

On Privatization

A focus on private affairs, personal problems, and psychological processes—we can surely see the effects of privatization in the great majority of the sermons studied here. First, in its sense of limiting religious speech to matters of private concern, privatization occurs as the preachers draw lessons that are relevant to one's personal life, while ignoring the wider context of meaning.

In speech about God, notions of the deity as sovereign of the collectivity are displaced by portraits of God as Significant Other, who provides comfort, counsel, and understanding for the individual's psychological concerns. In talk about Christian conduct in the world, the human being is depicted largely in terms of a solitary path, whether taking the path results in challenge and enjoyment of the world's plural offerings, as in most Presbyterian sermons, or in alienation or "lostness," as in many Southern Baptist messages. In sermons that confront the traditional concept of sin, as well as those that transmute it into speech about errors in behavior, wrongdoing is frequently discussed as violations of personal satisfaction or family values, rather than as violations of community norms. In talk about conversion, the speech segregates individuals from the larger social group—not only, in some sermons, from formal organizations, but also, in many more, from even their most intimate human others, as the possibility of interpersonal fulfillment through human relationships is denied. The absence of messages about engaging in collective action is virtually complete, and there are few arguments about religious obedience or adherence based on community obligations or standards. Instead, in this speech, the private self of the individual is bounded away from the larger social collectivity.

If the limitation of focus in the sermons to the individual in isolation from the human community is noteworthy, there is another aspect of privatization that is equally hard at work: the transfer of truth claims from the objective world to the subjectivity of the individual. In its position of default—with its ability weakened to make claims about objective truths—religious speech is positioned as relevant for satisfying a person's psychological needs; hence the elaboration on the depths of the individual psyche. As the nature and the needs of the interior self are probed in the sermons, the inner workings of the individual are constituted as a complex arena of analysis, understanding, and change.

Apparently accepting the role assigned to religion as one of giving expert opinion on the individual's psychological needs, this speech further accepts some of psychology's secular assumptions:

· The self should be objectified and explored by individuals so that they can "work on themselves."
· The self is apprehended through subjective awareness, particularly through feelings, which, when acknowledged and objectified, become "knowledge."
· Success in the endeavor of self-knowledge and self- transformation may be measured subjectively, through the assessment of one's feelings.

These are underlying premises implicit in much Southern Baptist talk about motivations for and progress toward conversion, and in much Presbyterian speech about the growth and development of the self and feelings of joy and cheer over one's relationship with God.

Given the understanding of human selfhood that the language of psychology has contributed to contemporary religious speech, it is not surprising that God also is frequently characterized in terms of his internal states. We have seen God described in these sermons with respect to his thoughts, but even more so with respect to his feelings, particularly anguish and sorrow on behalf of his errant human children. Instead of rendering a transcendent God of majesty and power, many of the sermons depict God's psychological states and needs: the love he experiences for humankind in his role as daddy, the transparency of his longing for reunification with each individual person. If privatization has made it difficult for pastors to pose truth claims about objective realities—leaving only the realm of interior experience open to religious speech—it would seem reasonable that the God portrayed in the sermons would be configured by his subjectivity, just as human beings render and make sense of themselves.

How do human beings come to perceive and understand God in these sermons? With the decreasing plausibility of propositional claims about the nature of God comes a substitute, psychological claim: God is made plausible through the individual's emotional identification with him. Thus, we see elaboration on the shared experiences of God and human beings, as God opens himself up to pain on behalf of his son, just as human parents would suffer on behalf of their offspring, and as God readily communicates his love for humankind, just as men and women are urged to disclose themselves to God. God's emotional states so mirror ours that identification and communication are easily available.

The language of many of the sermons, however, does not merely restrict God to the realm of subjective apprehension; it also provides an important mechanism for the reinforcement and continuation of this practice. As this God speaks to our own subjectivities in reflecting them, he justifies our concern with them. The God created in this speech validates human beings' incessant interest in their private inner workings. God legitimates people's fascination with the depths of their emotional experiences. This is a God whose transcendent qualities have, for the most part, disappeared; a God who, in his immanence and understanding, smiles benevolently on the age of psychology.

132

On Pluralization

No longer an ideological monopoly, Peter Berger has argued, religion in the West has become a market commodity.[2] Pluralization has created a situation wherein multiple forms of religious and secular belief and practice become available, which must be sold to potential consumers. Thus, religions reconstruct themselves as consumer items, which compete with others in a marketplace of creeds and practices. As religious speakers accept the need to market their pronouncements, they tacitly ratify the capitalist notion of consumer choice.

As potential adherents are positioned as voluntary consumers, we would expect to see the persuasive marketing of religious ideologies. Indeed, positive inducements far outweigh threats for noncompliance in the sermons. Consonant with contemporary marketing practices, religion (the "product") is posed as an answer to consumer needs; religious adherence is seen as solving problems that arise in the psychological or practical everyday experience of men and women. When we examine the "benefits" of religion offered in the sermons against the backdrop of contemporary culture, we can see the problems that the benefits are meant to address. To counter the cold, calculating weight of bureaucratic impartiality, the sermons offer self-esteem regardless of the merit one actually earns. In the context of a modern world that presupposes one's need for intimacy, yet whose busyness and mobility make it difficult to attain, God is promised as a perfect interpersonal partner. In light of the uncertainties and complexities of contemporary pluralism, the speech holds forth the remission of anxiety and feelings of alienation. And as one's expressive side is dampened by the rationalization of modern work, the sermons teach people how to "get in touch" with their feelings.

At first glance, we might be tempted to read this list as a mixed discourse of accommodation and resistance. There seems to be a strain of resistance in the remedies of religion advertised above, since they are posed as counterweights to the practices of secularity—the substitution of feelings of intimacy and personal worth for the impersonality of the workplace and mass society, the injection of affect into a life of pervasive rationalism, and the provision of certainties in the face of the confusions of pluralism. Indeed, these remedies do suggest that religion is "something different," distinctive, in some respects, from the secular world.

But in fact, it would appear that the resistance of these formulations is severely compromised. First, the premise of religion as another ideological market commodity seems to have been accepted, as speakers give persuasive appeals about the benefits of their "product," and as they individuate their listeners as consumers (freed from obligations of traditions or collectivities) who make their own "purchasing choices." Second, the speech once again accepts the exile of religion into the region of private life, in its concerns largely for the psychology and affect of the individual. The solutions that are posed here to consumer "needs" are *privatized* counterbalances to modern life, minor irruptions in the overall secularity of the social world. These solutions do not challenge the adequacy of a definition of religion that limits its relevance to the private sphere. In effect, the speech of the sermons has conceded the point.

On Rationalization

As religious pronouncements accommodate to secular norms of rationality, we might expect to see a trend toward doctrines and instructions for behavior that embody norms of efficiency and effectiveness in reaching a desired goal. This is apparent in the tendency of many of the sermons to systematize the procedure of conversion, as the process of reaching conversion is framed as a series of steps instrumental for achieving that end. We even noted the change in speech style occurring at the point where these instructions were given, as the language of technical proceduralism replaced that of poetic evocation used in descriptions of human nature. The systematization of these instructions makes conversion efficient for the individual. The steps enumerated are presented as the most straightforward, time- and labor-saving, path toward the given end. As we have seen, these techniques are also presented in terms of their effectiveness: Comply with the instructions, the language suggests, and conversion will follow. Indeed, in some sermons, conversion is effected even as the listener's innate qualities and needs are described in the talk.

The rationalization of conversion applies not only to the individual adherent; it is also apparent on the level of the churches as a whole. From their point of view, the most efficient means to their end—marketing the benefits of religious adherence to as wide an audience as possible—is gained by articulating standardized appeals that are universally applicable. We see this operating not only through the speech of conversion procedures, but also as prior talk about human nature and human need has standardized the self. If people are fully constituted by their likeness, then universal techniques become possible, resulting in massive efficiencies of scale.

Akin to standardization of the self are other constructions in the speech which apparently are functional for the mass-marketing of religious adherence. Most obvious is the simplification of doctrine for mass consumption, as we have seen in the pastors' speech about God. First, as I pointed out, the Trinity—the precise configuration of whose nature was a matter of grave concern for theologians of the early church—has been collapsed in much of this speech into a single entity, an undifferentiated blend of the Persons. It is likely that this move has aided the tendency toward softening and mellowing God's transcendent characteristics, as the majestic remove of the Father gives way to the human qualities of the Son.

There is another way in which God's nature has been simplified in the speech of these sermons. Many of the sermons depict a God whose behavior is regular, patterned, and predictable; he is portrayed in terms of the consistency of his behavior, of the conformity of his actions to the single rule of "love." The listener always knows how God will act. This God is not subject to flashes of anger, unpredictable episodes of vengeance, or actions based on hidden reasons. True, in the sermons, God appears to act on the basis of emotion, not of reason; but his emotions are standardized, simplified according to a single norm of behavior, and thus easily comprehended. The simplification of doctrine about God's nature suggests a deity whose very regularity makes his behavior predictable, further insuring the rationalized effectiveness of conversion and of ongoing communication.

THE DISCOURSE OF RESISTANCE

Dramatic as the signs of accommodation are, some sermons also show evidence of resistance to secular culture. Theorists have suggested that moves toward religious accommodation spur countermoves in the direction of resistance. My examination of the language of the sermons allows us to see the multiple facets of this response. While other research tends to look at religious resistance as reassertion of traditional morality against the backdrop of its perceived erosion in late-twentieth-century American culture, and as political mobilization on behalf of that morality, my focus on the speech of the sermons sheds light on other aspects of resistance, those grounded more tightly in theology.[3]

The first aspect of resistance involves resacralization, the reinjection of sacred talk into religious pronouncements. Resacralization is visible in the sermons studied in this book in several ways.

First, and most important, many Southern Baptist and some Presbyterian sermons insist upon rendering a God-centered anthropology. This tendency is especially apparent as the sermons preach about an essential human nature in detailing the road to conversion. Here attributed to God's design for his creation, human nature is universal, essentially immutable, ultimately coherent, and the controlling core of the self. This view of human nature is a direct rebuttal to modernity's notion of the fragmented self. In addition, the view serves partially to deprivatize talk about the self as it renders human identity and need as "facts" external to the subjective awareness of the individual.

I am not suggesting that this speech comprises a pure discourse of resistance. Elements of accommodation are present in the talk as well, as the essentialist notions that ground human identity in human nature mingle with the language of contemporary psychology. But, although the talk acknowledges the migration of religion to the private sphere as it speaks of issues of psychological concern, the speech simultaneously insists on grounding doctrine in an objective nature of human beings, rooted in the act of divine creation.

This insistence rejects at least part of the moral framework of contemporary relativism on which psychological notions are based. Instead of assessing human behavior on a trial-and-error basis, consonant with the ambiguous principles of change or growth, and of seeking the results of good feelings, human behavior is anchored in a definition that lends itself to objectifiable criteria. In addition, Southern Baptist talk about conversion as a joint project between God and human beings serves to reject the assumption in modern psychology that individuals are free to craft themselves as they wish. Thus, although it does not completely resist the temptations of contemporary psychological notions of identity, this speech appears to provide a partial alternative to it.

Other, less marked elements of resacralization are also present in some of the sermons, although none remain uncompromised by accommodation. For example, we have seen the insistence in some sermons on traditional notions of sin, although we have also observed the ways in which sin is mitigated and deflected from application to listeners. We have seen the retention of some of God's transcendent qualities (particularly as some sermons discuss his judgmental role and others his quality of a-rational behavior), but we have also observed the relative weakness of these categories of speech. The impression one receives is that this talk is gingerly posed on a tightrope, simultaneously attracted and repulsed by the norms of secularity.

The second aspect of resistance entails building cohesion around core claims. We have seen minor elements of this practice in the occasional example of prooftexting, as biblical assertions are based on other biblical scripts. More important, cohesion is constructed in some sermons as they articulate natural-law understandings of cause and effect. As we have seen, this occurs when pastors talk about sinful conduct in the world, where the evidence for the wrongfulness of behavior is given by its visible, inevitably ruinous, results. Once again, the function of this device is to ground claims in an unchanging universe of objective truth. It is a guarantee of an orderly cosmos created and governed by divine principle and thus protected from the whims of purely human conduct.

The third aspect of resistance, the drawing of symbolic boundaries that separate truth from error and godly people from sinners, is present in the speech in two variations. In the stronger variation, it provides the exception to the privatized tendency in most of the talk. A small minority of Southern Baptist sermons suggest that human beings are not only solitary individuals accountable to God, they are also members of dichotomized communities of good and evil. In these sermons, the behavior of individual people has global importance, since their actions contribute either to protecting the community of purity from the pollution outside or relinquishing the community to the corruption of the world. In these highly charged examples, the pastors' speech works to constitute adherents as a sect, isolating them from external influences while strengthening internal bonds.

The structuring of symbolic boundaries is apparent in a weaker sense, too, where a vaguer notion of community is constructed. In this talk, as we have seen, some speakers separate the human world into categories of insiders and outsiders—those relieved from the charge of sinfulness (the sermons' listeners) and those who are used discursively to exemplify it (children, the underclass, and Jews). The resistance in this speech is not fully uncompromised, however. To be sure, as the talk functions implicitly to create categories of people in opposition to each other, it asserts the grounds for a classification scheme based on "objective truths" involving sin and godly behavior. Nevertheless, it can be argued that this talk is also motivated by a more accommodative concern: the ability to salvage some traditional doctrine about sin while at the same time, by buffering potential adherents from its force, following the marketing dictum, "never insult a customer."

THE DISCOURSE OF REFRAMING

I have suggested reframing as a possible alternative to the opposed strategies of accommodation and resistance. What evidence do we see of attempts to reformulate the role of religious language along these lines?

There are a few important examples of reframing in the sermons, which indicate the potential usefulness of this device within contemporary religious speech. The first occurs as some Southern Baptist preachers, in their speech about appropriate Christian life in the world, suggest that a person's existential dilemma is one of finding meaning in life. Thus, the role of religion is not so much to signify objective truths—such as teaching one to enjoy the offerings of life, as in much of Presbyterian speech, or presenting doctrines about salvation, as in some conservative Southern Baptist talk—as it is to provide the symbolic resources through which a human being may weave a coherent narrative about life, supplying overarching significance.

The speech strives for a middle ground between subjective and objective grounds of truth. On the one hand, it uses the language of psychology to speak to people's sense of alienation in the modern world. On the other, it suggests that the problems of alienation, which stem from separation from God, reach beyond the purely subjective into an objective state of being.

In addition to redefining the role of religion in the modern world, a few other preachers highlight the symbols modern practitioners might use to achieve overarching meanings about their Christian lives, without attaching the symbols to objective meanings. For example, as we have seen, one speaker centers human identity around the core, defining symbol of Christ, as he speaks of simultaneously viewing Christ's face in one's own true face—and vice-versa—in the recognition of one's authentic personhood. For another pastor, it is the overarching symbol of the cross that unifies the interpretation of one's life and dramatizes the ubiquity of God. And for a third pastor, life derives its meaning through the symbol of God's grace, evoked in the talk through a series of intertwined metaphors that suggest the ways in which language might be used to construct significance without attachment to a specific doctrine.

The evidence of reframing within these sermons is slim. But I suspect this speech style will come to be used more frequently in the future, for several reasons: as ongoing debates about inclusion in Protestant denominations call explicit attention to the constitutive power of language; as churches recognize the costs of unalloyed accommodation; and as attempts to resolve tensions between moderates and conservatives make salient the idea of striving for some middle ground.

Some Final Observations

A study that focuses on the complexities of language use would be remiss if it reduced findings to pronouncements "in the final analysis." But I would like to share some closing observations and speculations about the future of research in religious language and the place of religion in the modern world.

First, I hope I have adequately shown the usefulness of examining religious talk for the study of secularization. In addition to giving substance to theorists' categories and providing empirical evidence for the state of religion in modern times, a side benefit of discourse analysis lies in its ability to demonstrate the creativity, skill, and power of the preacher's art, conducted with extreme dexterity under trying cultural conditions.

Second, on a more substantive note, we have seen the range of discourses represented here. Certainly there are differences between Presbyterians and Southern Baptists, particularly concerning retaining traditional aspects of speech about sin and the qualities of God's transcendent face. But there are also apparent differences in speech style within each denomination, giving weight to Robert Wuthnow's assertion that the most important contemporary cleavages may be within, not between, denominations.[4] Whatever else we might wish to conclude, it seems clear that, although denominational boundaries still operate with respect to ideological pronouncements, they are no longer fixed entities, and indeed, are in the process of giving way to newer alignments.

Third, we have indeed noted the extent to which accommodative speech is used in the sermons. Various indicators point to the substantial adaptation of religion to the norms of secular culture. For all that, however, the accommodation is incomplete, whether it is viewed from the perspective of the sermons as a whole or an individual message. For religious speech still survives as a *religious* speech register; even in the seemingly most accommodated sermons, talk about God and about ultimate meaning endures at the center of concern. This may provide additional evidence that the persistence of religion on the American scene is in part connected with the ubiquitous social need for transcendent coherence and meaning, which may set limits to the degree to which accommodation may take place.

Fourth, despite what I have just said, some of the findings would appear worrisome to those who take seriously a central role for religion in modern life. We have noted the tendency of many of the sermons to downplay "negative" aspects of Christian belief and practice. As functional as this may be for selling religion in a contemporary context, we might wonder whether this speech has sacrificed some of its most important distinctive qualities, its singular contributions to the task of making sense of the human condition. What, for example, of the immensely potent Protestant doctrine of grace, which appears eviscerated in much of the speech as speakers fail to acknowledge notions of human depravity and separation from a transcendent God? What of the ability of religious speech to deal with concerns of theodicy, if it declines to contend with issues of human suffering and evil? What of the possibilities for creating and sustaining stable, binding communities of faith, if incentives to congregation are based purely on mutable perceptions of self-interest? If it loses these features and capacities, I think, Protestantism also loses its essential identity.

Finally, having noted the risks of extreme versions of religious accommodation, I believe it is important to recognize that all three responses—accommodation, resistance, and reframing—are necessary and useful styles of religious speech in the context of secularity. The response of accommodation at least allows for some continuity of religious tradition to be plausibly voiced in the isolating, fragmented culture of modern life. The response of resistance ensures that the language of supernatural religion and Scripture is not lost in modernity's Babel, reminding men and women that not everything is, or ever will be, under their control. And the response of reframing suggests the grave responsibility that practitioners accept when they speak of matters of religious concern, as they symbolize, and thus create, overarching meaning to their lives.

❖ Appendix One ❖

BRIEF HISTORIES OF THE TWO DENOMINATIONS

The Presbyterian Church (U.S.A.)

The current differences of theological and definitional opinion within the Presbyterian Church (U.S.A.), discussed in chapter one, were foreshadowed by a long denominational history of doctrinal disputes, internal quarrels, and schism. A Reformed tradition rooted in a strict interpretation of Calvinism, Presbyterianism began its institutional life in the United States with the founding of the first presbytery in 1706.[1] Not long after the burgeoning denomination was theologically organized by adoption of the tenets of the Westminster standards (1729), its ranks were split as the sweep of the First Great Awakening challenged traditional Calvinist notions of the relationship of the individual to church and God.[2] Theological conservatives—the "Old Side"—opposed the personal and emotional revivalism of the Awakening, hewing to formulations that maintained the centrality of the corporate church to issues of salvation. In contrast, the theological innovators of the "New Side" pronounced the importance of the inner experience of the individual person in the conversion event, unmediated by any person or institution.[3] The acrimony between the two groups over these theological issues and related concerns about the training of clergy led, at the middle of the eighteenth century, to a split that lasted over a decade.[4] In the interim, the New Side evangelized the Mid-Atlantic region, leading to marked gains in membership, and founded a college for the training of pastors (later, Princeton University). The influence of the New Side was sufficiently strong that the groups reunited in 1758 with considerable concessions to the innovators.[5]

Vigorous evangelistic efforts continued after the Revolutionary War. Presbyterians enjoyed a period of great membership growth in frontier areas and in the South as a result of the religious revival that ushered in the Second Great Awakening. A price was paid for this success, however. As evangelistic preachers modified the denomination's theological tenets and adapted their own preaching methods to make them more consonant with the requirements of converting large numbers of people through revivals, the resulting erosion in Calvinist doctrine lay the groundwork for future doctrinal disputes.[6] These adaptations included simplifying the complexities and theological refinements of the Westminster Confession and some modification of doctrine in the direction of Arminianism (the belief that human beings can, of their own free will, work toward their salvation). Further territory for contention over doctrine

141

was plowed by the adoption, in 1801, of the Plan of Union—a cooperative home-missionary venture with northern Congregationalists, whose theology was more liberal than that of traditional Presbyterianism.[7]

Thus, matters were readied for another controversy and resulting schism. In the early years of the nineteenth century, theological battle lines were drawn between the "Old School"—once again, forces of conservation which clung to a relatively orthodox version of American Calvinism—and the "New School," a group of theologians who, in line with evangelical experience and Enlightenment philosophy, denied the traditional doctrine of original sin and moved further in the direction of Arminianism.[8] A showdown in 1837 led to division between the two factions, and each new church eventually took with it about half the total membership.[9]

It was the issue of slavery, not specifically theological matters, that prompted a realignment of Presbyterian factions around and after the time of the Civil War. Major fractures in Presbyterianism occurred along regional lines, as the Presbyterian Church in the United States of America formed itself out of a reunification of the northern constituencies of the Old and New Schools, and the southern branches of the schools formed the Presbyterian Church in the United States.[10] In subsequent decades, each group followed a different theological course. The southern church, with a preponderantly white, relatively homogeneous membership, insulated itself from internal theological disputes by keeping aloof from social issues and accepting and acting on the basis of conservative theology and practice.[11] The northern church, while still predominantly conservative, gave ear to the growing liberal message: a doctrine with a high degree of Arminianism, stressing the free will of human beings and their capabilities for altruistic and ethical behavior; a depiction of God highlighting his immanent qualities; and an attitude of optimism about the ability of human beings to right the wrongs of the social world (leading some liberals to subscribe to the Social Gospel).[12] The resulting pressures between liberal and conservative factions of the northern church early in the twentieth century led to its involvement in the fundamentalist-modernist controversy after World War I.

Once again, issues in this controversy highlighted the extent to which Presbyterianism has been caught up in the swings of the theological pendulum over the years. In this case, although official church doctrines were modified in the early years of the twentieth century to acknowledge the Arminian position on free will, toning down traditional doctrines of predestination, the General Assembly (the denomination's governing body) promulgated doctrines that aligned the church with fundamentalism, in particular, the doctrine of biblical inerrancy.[13] Liberals responded with a condemnation of this doctrine, and the stage was set for debate and recrimination. But it was clear by now that, despite the publicity given to the fundamentalist turn that some factions had taken, the denomination as a whole would not rupture over this issue. In 1927, the General Assembly declared that no central group had the authority a priori to establish the essentials of faith, including the literal interpretation of the Bible.[14] This opened the door to a more pluralistic reading of Scripture by individual presbyteries and churches.[15] The more extreme fundamentalist wings left the denomination of their own accord, while the main wing of Presbyterianism sought a more moderate position of conservative evangelicalism.

The next theological development of major importance to Presbyterianism was the neo-orthodox response to extreme conservatism and, perhaps more directly, to liberalism. Although the dominance of this theological turn was short-lived (it did not fully enter American religious life until the mid-1930s and on the wane by the 1960s), neo-orthodoxy lent its distinctive vocabulary to Presbyterian speech. Its theology aided formulations in the northern church's Confession of 1967, which found a middle ground with respect to biblical authority in declaring that the Bible is not inerrant, and, thus, is subject to contextual and literary analysis; but that it was "given under the guidance of the Holy Spirit."[16] Neo-orthodox theology linked liberal concerns with social action to a more guarded view of the possibilities of human progress, urging churches to engage in constant self-reflection and to remain mindful of human dependence on God. And it called renewed attention to traditional Protestant concepts of human sinfulness and divine transcendence, while rejecting some of the extreme language of Calvinism. To a lesser extent than in the northern church, the language of neo-orthodoxy marked doctrinal statements of the southern church (the Presbyterian Church in the United States) as well, although their teachings remained basically conservative during this period.[17]

The language of neo-orthodoxy, however, was to lose ground to the rapid theological developments of the 1960s, 1970s, and 1980s. Consonant with moral and political changes in the larger American culture, this period saw the influx into Presbyterian speech of various politicized theologies, which called attention to the problems of blacks, women, lesbians and gays, and other nondominant groups.[18] The early part of this period also marked the highwater point of social action within the denomination, as liberal and radical clergy engaged in the civil-rights and anti-war movements. Indeed, at this juncture, clergy and church officials apparently moved further to the left in their theological attitudes and practices than did the laity. Cleavages appeared once again, this time not between sparring factions of theologians or clergy or laypeople, but between congregants and the pastors and denominational administrators who led them.[19]

Complicating the difficulties of finding consensus within the denomination were two important mergers—that between the Presbyterian Church (U.S.A.) and the United Presbyterian Church in North America, in 1958, and the larger consolidation of the northern church and the southern (the Presbyterian

Church in the United States) into the current Presbyterian Church (U.S.A.) in 1983.[20] Each merger brought different constituencies together, with their varied experiences and theological commitments, into a larger body already challenged by disagreement.

Another development within American Protestantism in this period deserves mention: the change in pastoral work that led to incorporation of modern psychological terms into theological pronouncements. As the influence of various strands of psychological thinking—in particular, the humanistic counseling style of Carl Rogers—took hold in the larger culture in the 1950s and beyond, they left deep marks on Protestant belief and speech. The focus in this talk on concerns of the inner self—its feelings and experiences, its authentic realization through growth and development—appeared to renew, in some quarters, or supersede, in many others, traditional speech about sin and disobedience to God. As some Presbyterian speakers found themselves engaged in the ideologies of "self-realization" and "self-acceptance," they bolstered the growing movement in some quarters toward theologies of cultural diversity, relativism, and tolerance. These theologies could only conflict with those of adherents who sought a more orthodox vision of Presbyterianism.[21]

THE SOUTHERN BAPTIST CONVENTION

Contemporary Southern Baptists are also descendants of Calvinism, but their special theological emphasis and their social experiences in America have taken them on a path far different from that of Presbyterians. The first Baptist church in the United States was founded by Roger Williams, the dissenter from Massachusetts Puritanism who fled to Providence, Rhode Island, in 1639. Further migrations from England in the mid-seventeenth century laid the groundwork for a Baptist presence in the colonies. Holding fast to distinctive beliefs and practices (for example, rejecting infant baptism in favor of the baptism of regenerate persons by total immersion), the Baptists underwent persecution at the hands of the Puritan majority.[22] Like other dissenting groups, the early American Baptists stressed the principle of religious liberty, in addition to more commonly held Calvinist creeds, such as the inerrancy of Scripture and the responsibility of the individual for conduct vis-à-vis God and the community. These tenets marked a core of Baptist belief despite other theological differences among Baptist immigrants from England and Wales later in the seventeenth and early eighteenth centuries.[23] "Particular" Baptists—those holding a Calvinist view of predestination—settled in New Jersey and Pennsylvania, while immigrants to Virginia and North Carolina adopted a more "General" theology, one that held out the availability of salvation to all.[24]

The First Great Awakening was a boon to Baptists as well as Presbyterians. Membership increased in the North and in the frontier South. In New England, revivalist zeal sometimes touched even entire churches of Congregationalists as members accepted second baptism and the church itself assumed the Baptist name.[25] The migration of large numbers of Congregationalists into Baptist churches was to continue for another half-century. In addition to swelling Baptist membership in the North, these conversions were instrumental in gaining southern adherents, as preachers in the northern Baptist churches (the "Separatist" Baptists) lent their talents to evangelizing the South. There, preachers replicated the fervor of the New England Awakening. With the help of local talent—southern farmers who became converted, heard the "call" to preach, and subsequently ministered to spontaneously-arising local congregations—Baptists were extremely successful in gaining converts.[26] In subsequent years, the emotional and dramatic tone of Separatist-style revivalism, along with the Separatist insistence on strong behavioral norms, had a far-reaching effect on Baptist beliefs and practices. This was true even though the Separatist yielded their nominal identity in a union with other Baptist churches in the late eighteenth century.[27]

Championing the idea of religious liberty, Baptists flocked to the Colonialist cause during the Revolutionary War. After the war, they devoted themselves to missionary efforts, which would become the hallmark of Baptist activity.[28] The first national organization of Baptists, established in 1814, was a foreign missionary society, quickly followed by other missionary associations.[29]

The Baptist presence was strong in the advance wave of revivals that ushered in the Second Great Awakening, particularly in the South and other frontier areas.[30] Unhampered by the educational and administrative requirements that sometimes encumbered Presbyterian revivalism, Baptist evangelism exploded during this period, as it promulgated the message of individual salvation and the autonomy of local churches. The very success of the revivals, however, coupled with an aggressive policy of foreign missionary activity, caused internal friction. Some churches objected to the Baptist missionary thrust, dissenting from the Arminian theology assumed by the revival and from the very idea of a central organization.[31]

By the 1830s, the monumental issue of slavery could no longer be ignored, and the opposing tendencies of northern and southern Baptist congregations foreshadowed a lasting rift. This was coupled with sectional disputes over methods of organization and the funding of missionary activity.[32] Matters came to a head in 1844, in a test case brought to the Home Mission Society concerning the appointment of a slaveholder as a missionary and in a request for clarification of missionary appointment policies. Angry about rulings that seemed to favor abolitionist interests, delegates from various Baptist groups in the South met in 1845. The Southern Baptist Convention (S.B.C.) was born out of the breach, in the region that would become coterminous with the Confederate States.[33] Yet, even after the war, despite another surge in membership growth, the fledgling organization remained a loose collection of local churches linked mainly with regional associations.

A major doctrinal dispute over issues of authority and identity dogged the S.B.C. at this time. Questions arose about the autonomy of the local church, the appropriateness of an overarching organization, and Southern Baptist cooperation with other denominations. Adherents of the Landmark movement—which, by the 1850s, had became fairly large and well-organized—held that they were the heirs to an unbroken succession of Baptists from the time of John the Baptist, and thus were the "true church." This meant that they were not required to cooperate in any way with the larger Baptist movement or with any other Christian (or secular) organization. They also disputed the propriety of overarching Baptist organizations, such as that overseeing the missionary effort, as an infringement on the rightful autonomy of the local church.[34] In addition to placing obstacles in the way of building a larger organization just as the S.B.C. was coming into being, the Landmark movement prefigured disputes over notions of Baptist identity and collaboration with other Protestant churches that were to arise in the future.[35]

At the end of the Civil War, many black Baptists in the South left their segregated quarters within white churches and later formed their own national association. About the same time, the S.B.C., which had been struggling during Reconstruction with the northern Baptist churches for control of missionary efforts in the South, began to resist northern efforts and assert its own associations.[36]

The period following Reconstruction saw continued growth for Baptist missionary work at home and overseas. Many Southern Baptists supported the Prohibition movement with the same evangelical zeal that fed their missionary labors.[37] With success in this area, Southern Baptists sought control over their own educational materials, which until then had been provided by the northern American Baptist Publication Society. In 1891, after a protracted struggle, the Sunday School Board was founded.[38] The board's influence far exceeds its modest name, since it serves as an agent through which a consistent Southern Baptist ideology can be promulgated to local churches.

Largely because of the S.B.C.'s high degree of theological, cultural, and demographic homogeneity, it was not affected as much by the fundamentalist-modernist controversy as was the Northern Baptist Convention.[39] Throughout the period, as in previous decades, the doctrine of biblical inerrancy was confirmed, though not without debate. In 1925, the doctrine was finally made official, in the first institutional confession of faith ever promulgated by the S.B.C. The document that was adopted states that the Bible is "divinely inspired . . . without any mixture of error for its matter."[40] Although some conservatives from the Northern Baptist Convention, displeased with the battle raging there, separated off and joined the S.B.C., some of the more extreme fundamentalist leaders within the S.B.C. departed, taking their followers off to smaller Baptist groups and independent Bible churches.[41]

The S.B.C. continued to increase the scope of its organization through World War II and afterward, expanding into the American West. During the next twenty years, the denomination spread to every state of the Union. This move, combined with demographic trends in the larger society, changed the profile of S.B.C. membership. Whereas, before this time, the typical S.B.C. adherent was a rural lower-class southerner, the new member could be a middle-class person, even a professional, who lived in a city or suburb in regions other than the South.[42] Eventually the shifting population base contributed to the S.B.C.'s confrontation with the forces of secularity, a development that led the denomination to a near-schism in the late 1980s.

The seeds of the current conflict were sown in the clash with the larger American culture. Previously sheltered by southern insularity and homogeneity, the S.B.C. was forced to come to grips in the 1960s both with the plurality of lifestyles and educational philosophies in the modern United States, and with developments that were specific to theology, especially the techniques of higher criticism in biblical interpretation that had been flourishing for years in liberal denominations. Battle lines were soon drawn within the S.B.C. over the inerrancy of Scripture, focused on issues of the interpretation of the book of Genesis that led to acrimonious doctrinal disputes in the 1960s and 1970s.[43] Another issue with the potential for fracture came as a movement of young Southern Baptists engaged in social activism over segregation in the churches and in the larger southern culture, and in protest against the war in Vietnam.[44]

Frustrated by what they saw as defection from traditional standards by some groups within the denomination—a sentiment aggravated by the relatively lax enforcement on the part of the S.B.C.'s agencies of certain conservative policies that had been voted in at annual meetings—a group of conservatives met in the mid-1970s to organize in protest against the alleged drift to the left of the S.B.C.[45] This movement, which rallied under the banner of fundamentalism, wrested control of the presidency of the convention. The group continues to lead the S.B.C. as of this writing. Previously viewed as an honorific post, the presidency has become extremely powerful in the hands of the fundamentalists, as incumbents have used the position to set the direction of the entire S.B.C. From this power base fundamentalists have guided the theological and practical agendas of the denomination. They have determined doctrinal standards for employees of S.B.C. agencies, and have even influenced the staffing of some seminaries along fundamentalist lines.

Although the hegemony of fundamentalists appears firm, theirs is not the only voice within the S.B.C. As Ammerman has shown, many laity and clergy in the S.B.C. disagree with the leadership even on some of the fundamentalists' key theological tenets—matters such as the inerrancy of the Bible, its sufficiency for all knowledge, and belief in premillenialism. When measured on a scale designed to gauge distance from or nearness to fundamentalist beliefs, the faith of the majority of adherents in the S.B.C. appears to fall within a large, somewhat diffuse range of conservatism, agreeing with some tenets of fundamentalism (such as biblical inerrancy) but rejecting others (such as the need for a strictly literal interpretation of Scripture). In addition, Ammerman found, a full 80 percent of Southern Baptist respondents identified themselves as conservatives, rather than as fundamentalists or moderates.[46]

More strongly dissenting views are found among the approximately 10 percent of respondents who call themselves moderates. Many reject the idea that the Bible is inerrant and should be interpreted literally, favoring, instead, toleration toward different hermeneutical practices in the denomination. Similarly, they support the notion of the "priesthood of all believers," repudiating the fundamentalist idea that pastors should have control over their churches. A large majority of those moderates polled by Ammerman supported the ordination of women, which is anathema to fundamentalists.[47] The more vocal among the moderates have organized themselves in opposition to the fundamentalist leadership; whether they can muster sufficient strength to take over from fundamentalists remains to be seen.

And so, at this juncture, the S.B.C. has lost the relative uniformity of culture that once characterized the denomination. Along with the Presbyterian Church (U.S.A.), which has confronted for some years already the challenges of religious faith in a secular word, the S.B.C. must reach into the resources of its heritage and contemporary invention alike to take a stance, whether of accommodation, resistance, or reframing of issues—or a mix of these three strategies—to the offerings and dilemmas of modernity.

❖ *Appendix Two* ❖

METHODOLOGY

In the spring of 1988, I wrote to pastors of 150 Presbyterian (U.S.A.) churches and 150 Southern Baptist churches in the United States, requesting a recent sermon on Luke 15:11-32. The churches were chosen by drawing a random sample of Presbyterian churches with memberships of over 800 persons from the roster of Presbyterian Church (U.S.A.) congregations (*Minutes of the 198th General Assembly*, 1986), and for Southern Baptist congregations, by random sampling of churches with memberships of over 1,000 people (drawn for me by the Southern Baptist Sunday School Board). The discrepancy in church size was necessitated by the organization of Southern Baptist records. It does not markedly affect the sample, however, since the majority of churches listed as having a membership of over 800 actually have memberships in excess of 1,000.

In all, twenty-seven Presbyterian and thirty-one Southern Baptist pastors sent a total of seventy-one sermons. Twenty-four of these sermons (thirteen Southern Baptist and eleven Presbyterian) could not be used in this study, for the following reasons: Six were outlines too sketchy to be analyzed; thirteen were manuscripts or tapes from pastors who sent several sermons (in that case, only the first sermon sent by each pastor was used in the analysis); three were tapes of messages that were not on the topic of Luke 15; and two were tapes that contained large sections that were inaudible.

Of the forty-seven usable sermons—twenty-one Southern Baptist and twenty-six Presbyterian—nine arrived in the form of audio tape and were transcribed by an assistant. The rest came in manuscript form or as complete outlines.

In addition to the sermons received, fifty-one Presbyterian and thirty-three Southern Baptist clergy responded to my request for sermons by writing that they had no such sermon on hand.

Methods of Analysis

I used two sets of discourse-analytic procedures in studying the text of the sermons. The first, a procedure that relies on analytical induction, was helpful in the first stages of analysis in identifying major patterns of talk (topics and categories within the topics) that I discuss in chapters three through six (in chapter three, for example, the *topic* is talk about "God"; the *categories* are God as daddy, God as sufferer, God as extravagant lover of humankind, and God as judge). The second procedure, close textual analysis, guided my examinations of details of text once the topics and categories were defined.

Generating Topics and Categories

Discourse analysis comprises a group of methods for studying patterns, structures, and rules in talk and text.[1] While most discourse analysts examine naturally-occurring talk, especially conversation, a few apply the methods to the written language of texts.[2] The goals of discourse-analytic research may be to generate and test hypotheses about the rules governing types of talk or the functions of particular classes of utterances, or simply to describe language patterns in the material under study.

As in other forms of naturalistic research, in discourse studies the analytical scheme is generated from the talk or text alone, rather than being derived from a preexisting theory. In descriptive research such as mine, the researcher uses methods of analytical induction to identify major patterns (in this book, topics and categories) within the material to be studied. The methods lead the researcher through a series of progressively refined codings of the data.

Systematically working through the body of talk or text, the researcher initially names topics and categories provisionally as they appear. When utterances are found that do not fit the provisional classifications, the coding scheme is, in effect, falsified. New topic and category labels are then identified, which provide a match with the data assessed up to that point. The process is repeated until all the relevant data have been subsumed under topic and category labels.

Close Textual Analysis

Once the major topics and categories in the sermons were identified, I examined the language in detail to see how each formulation was achieved. Close textual analysis involves examining structures of speech in which rhetorical critics take special interest:

- Metaphors and similes (for example, "God is a daddy to us"). These tropes are frequently used to express central ideas, and they tend to "spin out" beyond themselves into larger clusters of imagery (for example, "God nurtures his children").
- Symbolic boundaries (for example, marking distinctions between the world of the Christian and the world of Sodom). These expressions are used to classify groups of people and their institutions, ideologies and behavior.
- Structures of formal and informal arguments (for example, in proof-texting or in arguments from analogy). These arrangements show how "facts" are constituted in speech.

- Stylistic devices like repetition, redundancy, qualification, and elaboration. These devices frequently mark subtle similarities and differences among ideas and show what is important or troublesome to speakers.
- Rhetorical absences (what is not said). These omissions can point out ideas taken for granted in particular discourse communities or mark notions automatically ruled out from expression.

With these rhetorical devices as guideposts, I assessed every utterance of every sermon, until I was satisfied that all important formulations had been found and characterized.

Reviewing and Rereviewing the Findings

Ultimately, the strength of qualitative research such as this rests on the overall coherence and meaningfulness of the story told. The discourse-analytic techniques used in this research require a complete fit between categories and data, which forces the analyst to test every thread against the weave of the larger garment, to place every assertion into an overarching whole. My expertise and experience in discourse analysis gave me confidence that I was responsibly employing analytical techniques to the texts. But religious texts carry a resonance that other cultural materials may lack—especially to a researcher herself raised in a religiously observant household and who remains convinced of the positive role of religion in modern life.

What, then, have my biases read into or edited out of the sermons? How can I certify the validity of my analyses and interpretations?

Guarantees, of course, have little standing in purely human affairs. But I can attest to steps I took which make me reasonably sure of my findings.

First, during the early stages of the analysis, I followed the practice of "freewriting," exploring ideas and problems as they arose in the texts in long, unstructured memos to myself. This practice turned out to be instrumental in revealing areas in which the presuppositions and claims of my own tradition spoke most demandingly. In the freewrites, I laid bare a good deal of accumulated assumptions and feelings about religious faith, obligation, practice, and community—my own and those of others. For as long as I have been studying aspects of Christian theology, I have been aware of the attractions the study offers me and the conflicts it poses. But this project represents my most concentrated experience in coming to grips with the ways in which my own religious background colors my perception.

To some extent, the mere deed of exposing areas of bias was helpful, since it marked places where I was obliged to carry on a "conversation with the text." An even more productive remedy was to share the analyses and findings with others—professors of sociology and religion; theologians; laypeople and clergy

151

of both denominations; colleagues and friends raised in Protestant traditions ranging from liberal to fundamentalist, and others who, like me, are Jewish scholars of Christianity. Through these discussions, I discovered and attempted to work through occasional areas of overreading and idiosyncrasy, tempered overstatement and understatement, and sometimes reassessed analyses in light of the communal understanding.

In addition, the two processes of dialogue showed me how I could use my stance outside the church as a strength in doing this work, at the same time as I feared it as a weakness. Many of my early conversations with the sermons ended with my wondering how a non-Christian could adequately describe, let alone understand, the essence of discourses which, though cognitively familiar, were experientially foreign. Yet like an anthropologist doing fieldwork in a vastly different culture, I learned that my lack of "lived experience" in Christian faith and practice meant that I could approach the sermons with less of a struggle to "make things strange" and with a smaller degree of worry that intimacy with their ideas would lead me to take utterances for granted. I could notice things insiders did not perceive as remarkable.

Thus, with the understanding that the pure neutrality of objectivity is never available in the social sciences, I strove to make this study as fair as possible to the sermons and the faith traditions from which they come. I hope it sheds some light for those of us, from various communities of faith, who are concerned with the role of religion in modern times.

❖ Notes ❖

CHAPTER ONE

PROTESTANT PREACHING IN CONTEMPORARY AMERICAN CULTURE

1. Delaware Valley Community Church, Yardley, Pa., April 1990.

2. For example, recent Gallup polls have found that nine out of ten Americans claim to believe in God; 60 percent affirm the importance of prayer in their lives; and 85 percent say that religion is "very" or "fairly" important to them. See Gallup and Castelli, *The People's Religion*, 45, 59.

3. For recent reviews of traditional theorizing about secularization, see Dobbelaere, "Secularization: A Multi-Dimensional Concept"; and Tschannen, "The Secularization Paradigm."

4. Berger, *The Sacred Canopy*, chaps. 5 and 6; Fenn, *Liturgies and Trials*, esp. chap. 1.

5. Weber, "Science as a Vocation," 143.

6. Luckmann, *The Invisible Religion*, 99–102.

7. Weber, "Science as a Vocation," 155.

8. See, for example, Demerath and Williams, *A Bridging of Faiths*.

9. Bellah, *Beyond Belief*, 42–44; Lindbeck, *The Nature of Doctrine*, 32–40.

10. In 1990, the latest year for which data are available, 2,649,073 persons were reported as adherents (approximately 1.4 percent of the U.S. population). The figure comes from a personal conversation with Norman Green, Association of Statisticians of American Religious Bodies. Members tend to be Caucasian (95.7 percent) and to have levels of income and education significantly higher than the national average. The median age of members is fifty-four years. Data are from Presbyterian Panel, *1991–1993 Background Report*, 20, 24, 28.

11. Wuthnow, *The Struggle for America's Soul*, 72.

12. Presbyterian Panel, *Background Report*, 18.

13. Wuthnow, *The Struggle for America's Soul*, 75.

14. Steinfels, "Presbyterians Reject Report on Sex."

15. The membership figure of 15,238,283 is for 1992. The income of Southern Baptists is at the national average; educational level is slightly above it. Slightly more than 2 percent of Southern Baptists are African-American. The membership figure was reported in a personal conversation with Pat Strum, Research Services Department, Sunday School Board of the Southern Baptist Convention. Data on income and education are from Southern Baptist Convention, *1990 Southern Baptist Constituency Study*, 2. Information on African-American membership comes from a personal conversation with Norman Green, Association of Statisticians of American Religious Bodies.

16. For fundamentalists in the Southern Baptist Convention, biblical inerrancy entails the belief that the original documents of Scripture are without error in any regard, from its religious and ethical contents to its account of science and history. However, while others in the denomination—conservatives and moderates—tend to agree with the claim that the Bible is inerrant, there is a good deal of variation on how they interpret that claim. Many, for example, do not believe in a literal interpretation of Scripture. See Ammerman, *Baptist Battles*, 74–75.

17. Steinfels, "Southern Baptists: Facing a Deep Rift."

18. Leonard, "Between the Times in the SBC."

19. On power, see, for example, Clegg, *Power, Rule and Domination*; Mumby, *Communication and Power in Organizations*; and Tompkins and Cheney, "Communication and Unobtrusive Control in Organizations." Concern with the creation of "knowledge" is particularly prominent in constructivist approaches to sociology of science, for example, Mulkay, *The Word and the World*; Gilbert and Mulkay, *Opening Pandora's Box*; and Lynch, *Art and Artifact in Laboratory Science*. On public policy choices such as abortion, see Condit, *Decoding Abortion Rhetoric*; and Luker, *Abortion and the Politics of Motherhood*. On American values, see Bellah et al., *Habits of the Heart*; Carbaugh, *Talking American*; and Varenne, *Symbolizing America*.

20. Ammerman, *Bible Believers*; Balmer, *Mine Eyes Have Seen the Glory*; Peshkin, *God's Choice*; Tipton, *Getting Saved from the Sixties*; and Warner, *New Wine in Old Wineskins*.

21. Hunter, *American Evangelicalism*, 73–101.

22. For example, Gallup and Castelli, *The People's Religion*; Gallup and O'Connell, *Who Do Americans Say that I Am?*; and Piazza and Glock, "Images of God and Their Social Meanings."

23. The underlying premise seems to be that cultic, African-American, or "backwoods" religions are "exotic" phenomena deserving of in-depth analysis, but that mainline Protestantism—our dominant, often taken-for-granted culture—has nothing to say worthy of our study.

24. For examples of studies dealing with single issues, see Barker, *The Making of a Moonie*; Bainbridge, *Satan's Power*; and Van Zandt, *Living in the Children of God*. For examples of linguistic analysis without reference to larger social issues, see B. Rosenberg, *The Art of the American Folk Preacher*; and Titon, *Powerhouse for God*.

25. Swidler, "Culture in Social Action"; Bellah et al., *Habits of the Heart*; Carbaugh, *Talking American*; Harding, "Convicted by the Holy Spirit"; and Wuthnow, "Religious Discourse as Public Rhetoric."

26. In terms of Calvinist theology, the words of the preacher are seen as the vehicle through which God addresses men and women and brings them to union with Christ.

27. Stout, *The New England Soul*, 4.

28. Ahlstrom, *A Religious History of the American People*, 415–35.

29. Concerning changing demographics, there is considerable recent interest in the preaching of women pastors in mainline churches. See, for example, Smith, *Weaving the Sermon*. The introduction of various liberation theologies into some liberal and moderate mainline churches has spawned concern with issues of authority in preaching, raising doubts about the ethics of the traditional sermonic monologue; alternatives such as the narrative and interactive sermon are gaining place in some denominations. See, for example, Lowry, *The Homiletical Plot* and *Doing Time in the Pulpit*; Steimle et al., *Preaching the Story*. On recent renewal of interest into preaching dynamics, see, for example, Eslinger, *A New Hearing*.

30. Jeremias, *Parables*, 128–32; Bailey, *Poet and Peasant*, 158.

31. Wuthnow, *The Restructuring of American Religion*, 197.

32. In addition, a purely textual analysis cannot capture listeners' oral responses to the preaching, should any occur. With the exception of a style some have termed "African-American preaching," this type of interaction is not characteristic of mainline preaching. None of the sermons in the sample show major rhetorical features of "African-American" preaching as it is described by Mitchell, in his *Black Preaching*.

33. I did not collect information on demographic variables of the pastors or their churches, so I cannot know for certain whether there are African-American or other nonwhite pastors among the sample whose sermons are studied here. Given the demographics of the two denominations as a whole (in 1990, the Southern Baptist Convention reported approximately 2.2 percent of its membership as African-American; the Presbyterian Church (U.S.A.), approximately 2.3 percent), it is a good assumption that there are few, if any, African-American pastors in the sample. The figures on African-American membership come from a personal conversation with Norman Green, Association of Statisticians of American Religious Bodies.

34. Ammerman, *Baptist Battles*, 131.

35. However, where it is appropriate, I have given a sense of the frequencies with which particular rhetorical formulations appear in the sermons.

36. Greeley, *Religious Change in America*, 97.

37. Gallup Organization, "How Can Christian Liberals and Conservatives Be Brought Together?" and "Jesus Christ in the Lives of Americans Today."

38. Hunter, *American Evangelicalism*, 91–99.

39. Would the findings be different if sermons of other mainline denominations were studied? So little empirical data exist on language use in Protestant practice that only speculation is possible. There appears to be no substantive reason why theological tradition, in itself, would protect churches from the influence of secularity on religious speech, for most groups. But it is possible that, all other things being equal, a liturgical orientation could provide a relative degree of protection against secular influences, as preaching and other

discursive practices take a back seat to the performance of ritual obligations. It is also possible that strong communal ties in particular faith traditions (such as in some African-American churches) could buffer congregants from some forces of secularity, such as privatization. On the latter point, see Roof and McKinney, *American Mainline Religion*, 90–91.

40. Jackson, "Building a Case for Claims about Discourse Structure."

41. Berger, *The Sacred Canopy*, 180.

42. Berger, *The Sacred Canopy*, 180.

43. I discuss this topic more fully in Appendix Two.

44. Katz, "A Theory of Qualitative Methodology," 139–44.

CHAPTER TWO
SECULAR CULTURE AND THE CHURCHES' RESPONSES

1. Berger, *The Heretical Imperative, The Sacred Canopy*, and *A Rumor of Angels*; Hunter, *American Evangelicalism* and *Evangelicalism: The Coming Generation*; Luckmann, *The Invisible Religion*; Bellah, *Beyond Belief*; Douglas, *Purity and Danger*; Lindbeck, *The Nature of Doctrine*; and Wuthnow, "Religious Beliefs and Experiences"; "Religious Discourse as Public Rhetoric"; *The Restructuring of American Religion*; and *The Struggle for America's Soul*.

2. For the first two categories, accommodation and resistance, I use Hunter's terminology (*American Evangelicalism*), and my discussion of accommodation is partially indebted to his discussion of modern evangelicalism (*American Evangelicalism* and *Evangelicalism: The Coming Generation*). Because sociologists have shown little interest in the empirical examination of speech devices of resistance, my discussion of this category is more tentative than that of accommodation. The speech style I call reframing is speculative, based on some recent theoretical writings.

3. Discussion of these social forces is a major topic of secularization theorists. In particular, see Bellah, *Beyond Belief*; Berger, *The Sacred Canopy*; Hunter, *American Evangelicalism*, and *Evangelicalism: The Coming Generation*; Fenn, *Toward a Theory of Secularization* and *Liturgies and Trials*; Luckmann, *The Invisible Religion*; and Wilson, *Religion in Secular Society* and *Contemporary Transformations of Religion*. For a useful synthesis, see Tschannen, "The Secularization Paradigm."

4. Berger, *The Sacred Canopy*, 133; Hunter, *American Evangelicalism*, 91; Luckmann, *The Invisible Religion*, 97.

5. Even arguments about abortion and creationism raised in public forums by fundamentalist and evangelical Christians tend to take on the speech registers of science instead of those of religion; see Wuthnow, *The Restructuring of American Religion*, 302. On creationism, see Numbers, *The Creationists*, esp. chap. 12.

6. Fenn, *Liturgies and Trials*, chap. 6.

7. Hunter, *American Evangelicalism*, 91–99.

8. Habermas, *Legitimation Crisis*, 119–20.

9. Berger, *A Rumor of Angels*, 111.

10. Holifield chronicles the influence of humanistic and precursor forms of psychology on Protestant pastoral counseling in the United States in *A History of Pastoral Care in America*.

11. These themes in contemporary American speech are the subject of Carbaugh's *Talking American*.

12. Weber, *The Protestant Ethic*, 77.

13. Davis, *Becoming a Whole Person*; McDowell and Day, *How to Be a Hero*.

14. Hunter, *American Evangelicalism*, 88.

15. Menninger, *Whatever Became of Sin?*

16. Caplow et al., *All Faithful People*, 92.

17. Wuthnow, "Religious Beliefs and Experiences," 10–32.

18. Bellah et al., *Habits of the Heart*, 221.

19. Berger, *The Sacred Canopy*, 134.

20. Berger, *The Sacred Canopy*, 144–53.

21. See Hoover, *Mass Media Religion*, esp. chap. 9.

22. The cult of perfectionism promulgates norms of diet, exercise, and other physical means of self-improvement, such as cosmetic surgery, which have been adopted by some segments of the contemporary American middle and upper class. That the cult of physical perfectionism is a potential competitor to religion appears to be recognized at a popular level. Here are two recent examples. The *Yardley News*, a Bucks County, Pa., weekly, ran a display ad in the spring of 1990 for a local evangelical church picturing a young woman, who obviously has just returned from an aerobics class, staring thoughtfully into a mirror in a locker room. The caption reads, "Why settle for slowing the clock when you can live forever?" In the second example, in an interview published in the January 13, 1991 issue of the *Philadelphia Inquirer Magazine*, social satirist M. G. Lord is quoted as saying, "The problem with [yuppies] is that they believe death is optional, that if you exercise enough and eat the right thing, you can hang onto your mortal coil indefinitely. . . . I'd prefer to have [my] death experience mediated by religion than by exercise."

23. The practice of "shopping around" for a denominational or religious affiliation is common among contemporary Americans. Recent Gallup polls show that four out of five Americans have attended services at a church or synagogue of a denomination or religion other than their own. A third of Americans have attended religious services in five or more different denominations or faiths. In addition, the practice of "denominational switching"—changing one's denominational affiliation from the faith of one's childhood—occurs frequently. Gallup polls report that one third of the U.S. Christian population has switched denominations at least once. One in five has switched at least twice, and one in ten, three times or more. These data are reported in Wuthnow, *The Restructuring of American Religion*, 88.

24. Schuller, *Believe in the God Who Believes in You*.

25. Berger, *The Sacred Canopy*, 146; Bryan Wilson, *Contemporary Transformations of Religion*, 15.

26. Berger, *The Sacred Canopy*, 112–13.

27. The phrase announces the theme of Cuddihy's *No Offense: Civil Religion and Protestant Taste*.

28. Berger, *The Sacred Canopy*, 139.

29. Berger, *The Sacred Canopy*, 148.

30. Wallace, "Rationality, Human Nature, and Society in Weber's Theory."

31. Hunter, *American Evangelicalism*, 91–99.

32. Hunter, *American Evangelicalism*, 91–99. Featured in the 1992 Christmas catalogue of a national evangelical book chain are such titles as *The One-Minute Bible* ("a daily Bible-reading program at which anyone can succeed") and *The Bible Promise Book* ("[Bible-reading] made easy [through] simple-to-use alphabetical listing of topics").

33. A recent study by the Gallup Organization reports that most Americans surveyed view God as "easy to understand." (Gallup and O'Connell, *Who Do Americans Say that I Am?*, 23, 105). Wuthnow suggests that such simplification helps maintain the belief, in the modern context, that one can readily communicate with God (*The Restructuring of American Religion*, 303), a topic I address in chapter six of this work.

34. For example, a recent New Testament translation by The American Bible Society restricts its language to a reading vocabulary of under 1,000 words. The simplification of liturgies into colloquial English has jolted some sensibilities. In *A Far Glory*, Peter Berger complains of a new rendering of the Anglican Book of Common Prayer into "prose resembling that of a mail-order catalogue" (96).

35. Marsden, *Fundamentalism and American Culture*, 118.

36. Hofstadter, *Anti-Intellectualism in American Life*, 119, 121.

37. For critiques of fundamentalism that I think are unduly harsh, see, for example, Barnhart, *The Southern Baptist Holy War* and E. Rosenberg, *The Southern Baptists*. For a more balanced view, see Ammerman, *Bible Believers* and *Baptist Battles*; Boone, *The Bible Tells Them So*; and Marsden, *Fundamentalism and American Culture*.

38. Marsden, *Fundamentalism and American Culture*, 15.

39. See, for example, Thomas Barnes, "A New Concept of Mass—A Rejection of Relativity."

40. Marsden, *Fundamentalism and American Culture*, 57.

41. Boone, *The Bible Tells Them So*, 24.

42. Boone, *The Bible Tells Them So*, 44.

43. See Ammerman, *Baptist Battles*, 107; Boone, *The Bible Tells Them So*, 94.

44. For examples of the breadth of this movement—its infiltration into fields of science, economics, and politics, as well as the humanistic disciplines of philosophy, literary studies, and rhetoric—see Herbert Simons, *The Rhetorical Turn*.

45. Bellah, *Beyond Belief*, 42.
46. Lindbeck, *The Nature of Doctrine*, 33.

CHAPTER THREE
GOD AS DADDY, SUFFERER, LOVER, AND JUDGE

1. These data appear in Gallup and Castelli, *The People's Religion*, 45, 56, 58–59. They are drawn from Gallup polls of the American population as a whole, not exclusively of Protestants. But since 57 percent of the Gallup sample indicated that they were Protestants, it seems legitimate to interpolate from the findings of the polls regarding American beliefs in God in general to the beliefs in God of American Protestants.

2. According to a 1981 Gallup survey, Americans ranked highest in proportion of those who professed belief in God of citizens of major western democracies, including the Republic of Ireland, Northern Ireland, Spain, Italy, Belgium, West Germany, Norway, Netherlands, Great Britain, France, and Denmark. On a total scale of religiosity—which included measures of weekly church attendance, belief in a personal God, importance of God in one's life, belief in life after death, obtaining comfort from religion, and whether the church responds to the spiritual needs of human beings—Americans rated 67 (out of 100), compared to, for example, 36 for Great Britain and 32 for France. Only the Republic of Ireland, with a score of 73, ranked higher than the U.S. on this index. See Gallup and Castelli, *The People's Religion*, 47.

3. Hatch, *The Democratization of American Christianity*, 162–89.

4. Ahlstrom, *A Religious History of the American People*, 415–35.

5. Holifield, *A History of Pastoral Care in America*, 198.

6. Hatch, "Christianity and Democracy."

7. Ahlstrom, *A Religious History of the American People*, 944–46.

8. Hunter, *American Evangelicalism*, 91–99.

9. See, for example, the survey analysis of Piazza and Glock, "Images of God and Their Social Meanings"; Greeley, *Religious Change in America*, 97; Nelsen, Cheek, and Au, "Gender Differences in Images of God"; and Roof and Roof, "Review of the Polls: Images of God among Americans."

10. Hunter, *American Evangelicalism*, 73–101.

11. All percentages from this point on in this chapter are calculated on the base of the thirty-one sermons in which God is a central topic of speech.

12. Talk specifically about Jesus occurs only when he is mentioned as the speaker of the parable, and in some discussions of conversion. The conflation of the Persons of the Trinity into one undifferentiated entity is itself evidence of the simplification of doctrine about which I wrote in chapter two, as potentially complex matters are "smoothed" for popular consumption.

13. Categories are not mutually exclusive; many sermons use more than one set of images. Thus the figures given here total more than 100 percent.

14. The following convention is observed for all quotations from sermons in this book: The denominational affiliation of the preacher from whose sermon the quotation is taken appears in an abbreviation, placed in brackets, at the end of the quoted material—[P] for Presbyterian, [SB] for Southern Baptist.

15. Some scholars argue that the practice of translating *Abba* as "daddy" rests on a failure to contextualize Jesus' language. In proper context, they argue, the word translates as "Father." See Pilch, "Your Abba Is Not Your Daddy."

16. It is possible, of course, that the word *judgment* is so heavily coded that it condenses the entire thought (that is, that the unconverted will go to hell upon God's judgment), and that those familiar with the community's speech would readily interpret the word that way. But we are looking here at speech directed specifically to the unconverted. Pastors are not likely to assume that all these people—who may even be strangers to the church—know the code. In their speech about other matters relevant to the unconverted—for example, how one goes about getting saved—the pastors spell things out in exacting detail. It seems plausible, then, that the relatively weak attention given to God's agency regarding damnation of sinners is more a matter of civility when addressed to potential adherents than an example of restricted code (see chapter five).

CHAPTER FOUR
IMAGES OF CHRISTIAN FAITH IN THE CONTEMPORARY WORLD

1. Berger, *The Heretical Imperative*, 2.

2. In two Presbyterian sermons, the capitalist norm of exchange is implicitly criticized as it is contrasted with God's free gift of grace (excerpts from these sermons appear in chapter three). I have not treated this talk as a separate category about the world because the sermons deal with the topic only briefly and indirectly.

The lack of attention to social concerns in these sermons seems remarkable, given what is known about the history of some aspects of Presbyterianism. It may be that the Parable of the Prodigal Son is more likely to invite commentary on a different set of issues. Or it may be that the tendency to deemphasize social concerns marks a new attitude of Presbyterianism as a whole, or one that is specific to the larger churches, in light of declining membership. In any case, this is a finding that deserves further attention.

3. From this point on, all percentages are figured on the basis of the thirty-three sermons in which imagery around the world occurs.

4. "Love" may, of course, be understood as a duty of the Christian life. Thus, the obligation to love others could be rendered as a serious demand on adherents, requiring them to reject secular stances of relations governed by exchange to live a life of charity toward other human beings. The Christian life could then be cast as a rejection of worldly norms concerning human conduct.

But in the overwhelming majority of sermons in this group, the injunction to love does not carry with it strenuous behavioral demands, particularly with respect to altering one's conduct regarding norms of the secular world. "Love" has two constitutive features in these sermons, neither of which entails arduous behavioral demands. First is the nature of love as forgiveness, rendered here as the injunction not to count others' sins (or errors) against them. As this is depicted in the sermons, it calls for a change in attitude and public demeanor, but does not demand material or spiritual sacrifices.

The second feature concerns the conduct of family relationships. One should raise one's children with "love," and in many sermons, loving one's children does indeed entail a set of behavioral demands (especially concerning the time one spends in "open" and "sensitive" communication). But even this duty to love is not depicted as demanding a profound reformation of behavior.

In addition, the notion of "love" is just as apt to occur in the context of receiving love and enjoying love (from God) as it is in terms of giving love to others. That it is the first, and not the second, usage of the term that is being communicated in the sermon is clear from its context (the speaker has just debunked notions of self-denial that are connected to the obedient, dutiful behavior of the older brother of the Parable of the Prodigal Son). So it is plausible to conclude that this sermon is actually talking about the pleasant experience of receiving love rather than about the duty of giving it.

5. To test the strength of the secular attitude toward life expressed in this excerpt, try substituting the phrase, "The goal of [insert the name of any humanistic philosophy—say, EST or Rogerian therapy]" for the phrase "The Christian life" in the last sentence, and see if the paragraph still makes sense.

6. I discuss the massive understatement of this and related formulations—that feeding pigs lacks dignity for a Jew—in chapter five.

7. In *Purity and Danger*, Mary Douglas writes: "Danger lies in transitional states; simply because transition is neither one state or the next, it is undefinable. The person who must pass from one to another is himself in danger and emanates danger to others" (116).

8. Once again I remind the reader of the reservation voiced in the first chapter, that the most conservative Southern Baptist preachers may be underrepresented in this sample.

CHAPTER FIVE
IMAGES AND MITIGATIONS OF SIN

1. Edwards, "Sinners in the Hands of an Angry God," 160.
2. Noll, "God in the Colonies," 103.
3. Hatch, *The Democratization of American Christianity*, 171.
4. McLoughlin, *Revivals, Awakenings, and Reform*, 113–18.
5. Ahlstrom, *A Religious History of the American People*, 845.

6. Ahlstrom, *A Religious History of the American People*, 763–79.

7. Ahlstrom, *A Religious History of the American People*, 780.

8. Marsden, *Fundamentalism and American Culture*, 159, 224.

9. Marty, *Protestantism*, 94; Ahlstrom, *A Religious History of the American People*, 938–42.

10. One obvious indicator is substitution in the sermons of euphemism and circumlocution for direct talk about sin. These formulations include "blowing it," "failing," "falling into a trap," "wasting yourself," "mean, ugly, and stupid deeds" and "being stuck." Causality for wrong behavior is attributed to being "mishandled," "taking your hands out of God's hands," and falling prey to mental illness ("having a narcissistic personality"). Some of the preachers in the study remark on the tendency of their colleagues (and maybe, on occasion, even themselves) to give short shrift to notions of sin, or to explain it away. One pastor notes the replacement of talk about sin with the dialect of popular psychobabble:

> Have you ever thought about all the [other words we use in place of] sin. . . . A mere mistake, a maladjustment, an environmental conditioning, a social faux pas, a complex, a frustration, a phobia, a fear, a neurosis. [P]

Similarly, another pastor castigates the tendency of "soft" liberal approaches to waffle about sin:

> Preachers have newer and more elegant ways of [talking about sin], but are they really saying the same thing? These days people are maladjusted, immature, maybe, or suffering from a guilt complex; however *lost* belongs to old-time, camp-meeting revival days and it is as outmoded as the parlor lamp and the buggy whip. [SB]

11. Hunter, *American Evangelicalism*, 84–91.

12. See Cuddihy, *No Offense*.

13. None of the speakers make the stronger case here about the descent of the prodigal son into the pigpen: To an observant Jew, association with a ritually unclean animal not only is repulsive, it is a defilement. One could argue that the young man's close contact with pigs in the story is itself a mark of sin—that it is not just a result of sin but part of the behavior of sin. Although they do not treat the topic in this context, a few Southern Baptist speakers do depict sin as objective defilement in a different context, namely when they talk about the secular world (see chapter four).

14. Recall that, in the context of Luke 15, the Pharisees overhear Jesus' recounting of the Parable of the Prodigal Son.

15. In another sermon, the same pastor tells another Holocaust story. This one is an emotional account of a mother who chooses to accompany her young son to the gas chamber and there die with him, because she wishes to ease his

fear. After the story is told in elaborate detail, the speaker gives the following commentary (I reproduce it in its entirety):

> Let that story burn itself into your heart—God is just like that! We gather all over the world today at this table because God loved us enough to send His son that "whoever believes in Him should not perish but have eternal life!"

Now the story can reasonably and legitimately be seen to illustrate the theology of divine sacrifice that constitutes the heart of the Christian message. On its own terms, the commentary does not appear inappropriate. But there is another layer of interpretation that begs to be given, especially by a clergy-person, concerning the unfathomable human cruelty and depths of human suffering and sacrifice that the Nazi Holocaust entailed. It is not only, plausibly, a story about God but, certainly, one about a population of human beings who underwent a profoundly evil experience. Not to say a single word about this fact, within the context of theological speech, is markedly to trivialize the experience.

One is left wondering what these two Holocaust texts are intended to do, within the context of the speaker's preaching. On the one hand, even to relate them is to serve the laudable purpose of asserting that the Holocaust actually happened, and of not allowing its events to be forgotten. Even the barest recitation of these narratives is a positive deed. Yet, at the same time, one may be left uncomfortably surprised by the morals that are drawn from these stories.

Is the point of the Holocaust to teach us solely that the Jewish victim should forgive, and that God suffered a sacrifice of his own? To leave the lesson at that is, I think, to suggest that there is little in the way of a common sense of moral outrage that Christians share with Jews. Another possibility, and one that is hardly more reassuring, is that a concern with human evil has little place in contemporary preaching, as obsessed as it appears to be with presenting Christianity in terms of its upbeat message. As we shall see, there is evidence in these sermons to indicate that this may be the case. I return to that topic in the concluding chapter.

16. Hunter, *American Evangelicalism*, 86.

Chapter Six
The Transformed Self

1. Augustine of Hippo, *City of God*, book 14, 295–322; Taylor, *Sources of the Self*, 138–9.

2. Holifield, *A History of Pastoral Care in America*, 97.

3. McLoughlin, *Revivals, Awakenings and Reform*, 74–78.

4. Holifield, *A History of Pastoral Care in America*, 137.

5. Taylor, *Sources of the Self*, 389.

6. Holifield, *A History of Pastoral Care in America*, 197.

7. Ahlstrom, *A Religious History of the American People*, 779–81.

8. Holifield, *A History of Pastoral Care in America*, 227.

9. Niebuhr, "Religious Realism and the Twentieth Century," 413; Tillich, *The Religious Situation*, 219–25.

10. Rogers, "A Theory of Therapy," 236–62.

11. See Holifield, *A History of Pastoral Care in America*, 324ff., for a detailed discussion. Some theological critics of Rogers include Clinebell, *Mental Health through Christian Community*, and Johnson, *Person and Counselor*.

12. Six Southern Baptist sermons provide exceptions to some tendencies noted in this chapter. They do not depict the main benefit of conversion as providing the psychological comfort of an intimate relationship with God. Instead, conversion is seen as the reinstatement of the correct, original relationship between God the Father and his human creation.

13. Rogers, *On Becoming a Person*, esp. "The Implications of Client-Centered Therapy for Family Life," 314–28.

14. Tertullian wrote, "The corruption of our nature is another nature having a god and father of its own, namely the author of that corruption. Still there is a portion of good in the soul, of that original, divine, and genuine good, which is its proper nature. For that which is derived from God is rather obscured than extinguished." In Tennant, *The Sources of the Doctrine of the Fall and Original Sin*, 333–34.

15. It is instructive to contrast these images with dominant Presbyterian formulations around the idea of the self—not considered in the main body of the text because they do not deal with conversion. If the major thrust of Southern Baptist speech is to marry tenets of humanistic psychology with essentialist talk about human nature, Presbyterians are far more likely to subscribe more fully to the pop-psychological language of "personal growth and development," as the individual human being "matures" to her full "potential." Thus, for these speakers, personhood is reached through a forward-moving process of working out one's identity to achieve its possibilities, not, as in Southern Baptist speech, through recollection and reclamation of one's essential identification. Growth of the self—leaving the past behind—is a virtual mandate in this speech, sometimes even mandated by God, as we see in these excerpts:

Freedom in the Christian sense means being free to be all that we can be—not bound by past mistakes, present weaknesses, or a too-small vision for the future; [P]

Many of us cannot face today or tomorrow because so much of who we are is anchored in yesterday. So many of our todays are ruined by the weight of yesterday; [P]

God wants us to move beyond the stereotypes and ingrained patterns to grow into a more satisfying way of living. [P]

The trajectory toward growth is only loosely coupled in this speech with the idea of one's relationship with God; while Christian principles may inform one's steps toward maturation, growth does not necessarily hinge on one's role as a child of God. With knowledge of the appropriate procedures (garnered from humanistic psychology) one may chart a course toward growth on one's own, as this speaker suggests:

> Thanks to the writings of the Menningers, Scott Peck, and others, we have some tools that can be used to track how well people are doing in this business of growing. . . . There are three "R"'s. Reality is the recognition of things as they really are. No rose colored glasses. No fantasy. . . . Responsibility is the active rather than passive participation in life. Making one's own choices and carrying one's own share of the load. . . . Relational maturity means a growing capacity to be open and honest in such a way that everyone is richer for it. [P]

16. Another type of appeal that one might expect to see in the sermons— exhortation to conversion based on fear of punishment in hell—appears relatively rarely (it is present in only seven Southern Baptist sermons) and is relatively weak in force where it does appear. In general, the idea of hell is left unelaborated: where it occurs, it is mentioned, but not described. Only one sermon comes close to detailing the suffering that the unredeemed might expect from eternal punishment, and, then, only in a brief passage. In other sermons, oblique references or euphemisms are substituted for the notion of hell, as in this pastor's genteel reframing:

> And that's why John told us that God so loved the world that he gave his own begotten son, so that whosoever believeth in him, should not perish—*let me change the word*—should not keep on being lost until lostness is permanent. (italics mine) [SB]

Other speakers debunk appeals to conversion based on fear, consonant, as we have seen, with denials that God behaves like Yahweh. For example, one pastor says:

> Grady Nutt used to say that he grew up in churches where the preacher so loved to preach on judgment that he felt like a hotdog dangling over the fires of hell each week. One can almost get the impression that God secretly anticipates the pronouncement of eternal doom on sinners. But the facts are that nothing is further from the truth. . . . Rather than desiring judgment, He desires salvation for them. [SB]

17. Listeners are buffered from the negative possibilities of failure or struggle in their *own* journeys toward conversion by the obliqueness of this and

similar texts, which deflect the idea of difficulties onto other people's experiences.

CHAPTER SEVEN
SECULARITY AND RELIGIOUS SPEECH IN THE TWO DENOMINATIONS

1. Wuthnow, "Religious Discourse as Public Rhetoric," 318.
2. Berger, *The Sacred Canopy*, chap. 5.
3. See, for example, Hunter, *American Evangelicalism*; and Liebman and Wuthnow, eds., *The New Christian Right*.
4. Wuthnow, *The Restructuring of American Religion*.

APPENDIX ONE
BRIEF HISTORIES OF THE TWO DENOMINATIONS

1. Lingle and Kuykendall, *Presbyterians*, 67.
2. Trinterud, *The Forming of an American Tradition*, 53.
3. Lingle and Kuykendall, *Presbyterians*, 68.
4. Trinterud, *The Forming of an American Tradition*, 107.
5. Trinterud, *The Forming of an American Tradition*, 148.
6. Ahlstrom, *A Religious History of the American People*, 444.
7. Marsden, *The Evangelical Mind*, 11.
8. Marsden, *The Evangelical Mind*, 43, 54.
9. Ahlstrom, *A Religious History of the American People*, 468.
10. Ahlstrom, *A Religious History of the American People*, 661.
11. Lingle and Kuykendall, *Presbyterians*, 84.
12. Ahlstrom, *A Religious History of the American People*, 775.
13. Ahlstrom, *A Religious History of the American People*, 814.
14. Loetscher, *The Broadening Church*, 134.
15. Rogers and McKim, "Pluralism and Policy in Presbyterian Views of Scripture," 38.
16. Moorhead, "Redefining Confessionalism," 68.
17. Moorhead, "Redefining Confessionalism," 72.
18. Moorhead, "Redefining Confessionalism," 78.
19. Wuthnow, *The Struggle for America's Soul*, 76.
20. Lingle and Kuykendall, *Presbyterians*, 76; Wuthnow, *The Restructuring of American Religion*, 165.
21. Holifield, *A History of Pastoral Care in America*, 354–56.
22. Brackney, *The Baptists*, 11.
23. Ammerman, *Baptist Battles*, 23.
24. Ahlstrom, *A Religious History of the American People*, 317.
25. Brackney, *The Baptists*, 13.
26. Ahlstrom, *A Religious History of the American People*, 323.

27. McBeth, *The Baptist Heritage*, 234–35.
28. Ammerman, *Baptist Battles*, 26.
29. McBeth, *The Baptist Heritage*, 344.
30. Ammerman, *Baptist Battles*, 27.
31. McBeth, *The Baptist Heritage*, 371.
32. Ammerman, *Baptist Battles*, 32.
33. McBeth, *The Baptist Heritage*, 386–88.
34. McBeth, *The Baptist Heritage*, 450.
35. Ammerman, *Baptist Battles*, 33.
36. McBeth, *The Baptist Heritage*, 789.
37. Ammerman, *Baptist Battles*, 38.
38. McBeth, *The Baptist Heritage*, 432.
39. Thompson, *Tried as by Fire*, 61.
40. Brackney, *The Baptists*, 30.
41. Ammerman, *Baptist Battles*, 49.
42. Ammerman, *Baptist Battles*, 54.
43. McBeth, *The Baptist Heritage*, 681.
44. Ammerman, *Baptist Battles*, 66.
45. McBeth, *The Baptist Heritage*, 683.
46. Ammerman, *Baptist Battles*, 77.
47. Ammerman, *Baptist Battles*, 97.

Appendix Two
Methodology

1. See Jackson, "Building a Case for Claims about Discourse Structure."
2. See, for example, Green, *Knowing the Poor*.

✦ Bibliography ✦

Ahlstrom, Sidney. *A Religious History of the American People*. New Haven, Conn.: Yale University Press, 1972.

Ammerman, Nancy. *Bible Believers: Fundamentalists in the Modern World*. New Brunswick, N.J.: Rutgers University Press, 1987.

————. *Baptist Battles*. New Brunswick, N.J.: Rutgers University Press, 1990.

Augustine of Hippo. *City of God*. Garden City, N.Y.: Image Books, 1958.

Bailey, Kenneth. *Poet and Peasant*. Grand Rapids, Mich.: Eerdmans, 1976.

Bainbridge, William Sims. *Satan's Power*. Berkeley: University of California Press, 1978.

Balmer, Randall. *Mine Eyes Have Seen the Glory: A Journey into the Evangelical Subculture in America*. New York: Oxford University Press, 1989.

Bangley, Bernard. *If I'm Forgiven, Why Do I Feel So Guilty?* Wheaton, Ill.: Harold Shaw Press, 1992.

Barker, Ellen. *The Making of a Moonie*. Oxford, Eng.: Blackwell, 1984.

Barnes, Thomas. "A New Concept of Mass—A Rejection of Relativity." In *Science at the Crossroads: Papers of 1983 National Creation Conference*. Richfield, Minn.: Onasimus Publishing, 1983.

Barnhart, Joe. *The Southern Baptist Holy War*. Austin: Texas Monthly Press, 1986.

Bellah, Robert. *Beyond Belief: Essays on Religion in a Post-Traditional World*. New York: Harper & Row, 1970.

Bellah, Robert, Richard Madsen, William Sullivan, Ann Swidler, and Steven Tipton. *Habits of the Heart*. New York: Harper & Row, 1985.

Berger, Peter. *The Sacred Canopy*. Garden City, N.Y.: Doubleday, 1967.

————. *A Rumor of Angels*. New York: Doubleday, 1970.

————. *The Heretical Imperative*. New York: Doubleday, 1979.

————. *A Far Glory*. New York: Free Press, 1992.

Boone, Kathleen. *The Bible Tells Them So: The Discourse of Protestant Fundamentalism*. Albany: State University of New York Press, 1989.

Brackney, William. *The Baptists*. New York: Greenwood Press, 1988.

Caplow, Theodore, Howard Bahr, Bruce Chadwick, Dwight Hoover, Laurence Martin, Joseph Tamney, and Margaret Williamson. *All Faithful People: Change and Continuity in Middletown's Religion*. Minneapolis: University of Minnesota Press, 1983.

Carbaugh, Donal. *Talking American: Cultural Discourses on Donahue*. Norwood, N.J.: Ablex Press, 1988.

Charmaz, Kathy. "The Grounded Theory Method: An Explication and Interpretation." In *Contemporary Field Research*, ed. R. Emerson, 109–26. Prospect Heights, Ill.: Waveland Press, 1983.

Clegg, Stewart. *Power, Rule and Domination*. London: Routledge & Kegan Paul, 1975.

Clinebell, Howard. *Mental Health through Christian Community*. Nashville, Tenn.: Abingdon Press, 1965.

Condit, Celeste. *Decoding Abortion Rhetoric: Communicating Social Change*. Urbana: University of Illinois Press, 1990.

Cuddihy, John. *No Offense: Civil Religion and Protestant Taste*. New York: Seabury Press, 1978.

Davis, Ron Lee. *Becoming a Whole Person in a Broken World*. Grand Rapids, Mich.: Discovery House, 1990.

Demerath, N.J. III, and Rhys Williams. *A Bridging of Faiths: Religion and Politics in a New England City*. Princeton, N.J.: Princeton University Press, 1992.

Dobbelaere, Karel. "Secularization: A Multi-Dimensional Concept," *Current Sociology* 29:1–215 (1981).

Douglas, Mary. *Purity and Danger*. New York: Pantheon Books, 1966.

Edwards, Jonathan. "Sinners in the Hands of an Angry God." In *Jonathan Edwards: Representative Selections*, ed. C. Fast and T. Johnson, 155–72. New York: American Book Company, 1935.

Eslinger, Richard. *A New Hearing*. Nashville, Tenn.: Abingdon Press, 1987.

Farley, Edward. "The Presbyterian Heritage as Modernism." In *The Presbyterian Predicament*, ed. M. Coalter, J. Mulder, and L. Weeks, 49–66. Louisville, Ken.: John Knox/Westminster Press, 1990.

Fenn, Richard. *Liturgies and Trials: The Secularization of Religious Language*. New York: Pilgrim Press, 1982.

———. *Toward a Theory of Secularization*. Storrs, Conn.: Society for the Scientific Study of Religion, 1978.

Gallup, George, Jr., and Jim Castelli. *The People's Religion: American Faith in the '90's*. New York: Macmillan, 1989.

Gallup, George, Jr., and George O'Connell. *Who Do Americans Say that I Am?* Philadelphia: Westminster, 1986.

Gallup Organization. "How Can Christian Liberals and Conservatives Be Brought Together?" Princeton, N.J., 1984.

———. "Jesus Christ in the Lives of Americans Today." Princeton, N.J., 1983.

Gilbert, G. Nigel, and Michael Mulkay. *Opening Pandora's Box: A Sociological Analysis of Scientists' Discourse*. Cambridge, Eng.: Cambridge University Press, 1984.

Greeley, Andrew. *Religious Change in America*. Cambridge, Mass.: Harvard University Press, 1989.

Green, Brian. *Knowing the Poor: A Case Study in Textual Reality Construction*. London: Routledge & Kegan Paul, 1983.

Groom, Nancy. *From Bondage to Bonding: Escaping Codependency, Embracing Biblical Love*. Colorado Springs: NavPress, 1991.

Habermas, Jürgen. *Legitimation Crisis*. Boston: Beacon Press, 1975.

Harding, Susan. "Convicted by the Holy Spirit: The Rhetoric of Fundamental Baptist Conversion." *American Ethnologist* 13:167–81 (1986).

Hatch, Nathan. "Christianity and Democracy: From the Revolution to the Civil War." In *Eerdmans' Handbook to Christianity in America*, ed. M. Noll, N. Hatch, G. Marsden, D. Wells, and J. Woodbridge, 159–276. Grand Rapids, Mich.: Eerdmans, 1983.

————. *The Democratization of American Christianity*. New Haven, Conn.: Yale University Press, 1989.

Hofstadter, Richard. *Anti-Intellectualism in American Life*. New York: Knopf, 1963.

Holifield, E. Brooks. *A History of Pastoral Care in America*. Nashville, Tenn.: Abingdon Press, 1983.

Hoover, Stewart. *Mass Media Religion*. Newbury Park, Calif.: Sage, 1988.

Hunter, James D. *American Evangelicalism: Conservative Religion and the Quandary of Modernity*. New Brunswick, N.J.: Rutgers University Press, 1983.

————. *Evangelicalism: The Coming Generation*. Chicago: University of Chicago Press, 1987.

Jackson, Sally. "Building a Case for Claims about Discourse Structure." In *Contemporary Issues in Language and Discourse Processes*, ed. D. Ellis and W. Donohue, 129–41. Hillsdale, N.J.: Lawrence Erlbaum, 1986.

Jeremias, Joachim. *The Parables of Jesus*. New York: Charles Scribner's Sons, 1954.

Johnson, Paul. *Person and Counselor*. Nashville, Tenn.: Abingdon Press, 1967.

Katz, Jack. "A Theory of Qualitative Methodology: The Social System of Analytic Fieldwork." In *Contemporary Field Research*, ed. R. Emerson, 127–48. Prospect Heights, Ill.: Waveland Press, 1983.

Kierkegaard, Soren. *Sickness unto Death*. New York: Doubleday, 1954.

Leonard, Bill. "Between the Times in the SBC." *Christian Century* (May 29–June 5, 1991).

Liebman, Joshua L. *Peace of Mind*. New York: Simon & Schuster, 1946.

Liebman, Robert, and Robert Wuthnow, eds. *The New Christian Right*. New York: Aldine, 1983.

Lindbeck, George. *The Nature of Doctrine: Religion and Theology in a Post-Liberal Age*. Philadelphia: Westminster, 1984.

Lingle, Walter, and John Kuykendall. *Presbyterians: Their History and Beliefs*. Atlanta: John Knox Press, 1988.

Lofland, John, and N. Skonovd. "Conversion Motifs." *Journal for the Scientific Study of Religion* 20:373–85 (1981).

Loetscher, Lefferts. *The Broadening Church*. Philadelphia: University of Pennsylvania Press, 1954.

Lowry, Eugene. *The Homiletical Plot: The Sermon as Narrative Art Form*. Atlanta: John Knox Press, 1980.

Lowry, Eugene. *Doing Time in the Pulpit: The Relationship between Narrative and Preaching*. Nashville, Tenn.: Abingdon Press, 1985.

Luckmann, Thomas. *The Invisible Religion*. London: Collier-Macmillan, 1967.

Luker, Kristen. *Abortion and the Politics of Motherhood*. Berkeley: University of California Press, 1984.

Lynch, Michael. *Art and Artifact in Laboratory Science*. London: Routledge & Kegan Paul, 1985.

Lyon, David. *The Steeple's Shadow: On the Myths and Realities of Secularization*. Grand Rapids, Mich.: Eerdmans, 1985.

Marsden, George. *The Evangelical Mind and the New School Presbyterian Experience*. New Haven, Conn.: Yale University Press, 1970.

―――. *Fundamentalism and American Culture*. New York: Oxford University Press, 1980.

Marty, Martin. *Protestantism*. New York: Holt, Rinehart & Winston, 1972.

McBeth, H. Leon. *The Baptist Heritage*. Nashville, Tenn.: Broadman, 1987.

McClure, John. "Changes in the Authority, Method, and Message of Presbyterian (UPCUSA) Preaching in the Twentieth Century." In *The Confessional Mosaic: Presbyterians And Twentieth-Century Theology*, ed. M. Coalter, J. Mulder, and L. Weeks, 84–108. Louisville, Ken.: Westminster/John Knox Press, 1990.

McDowell, Josh, and Dick Day. *How to Be a Hero to Your Kids*. Irving, Tex.: Word Books, 1991.

McLoughlin, William. *Revivals, Awakenings, and Reform: An Essay on Religion and Social Change in America, 1607–1977*. Chicago: University of Chicago Press, 1978.

Menninger, Karl. *Whatever Became of Sin?* New York: Hawthorn, 1973.

Mitchell, Henry. *Black Preaching*. New York: Harper & Row, 1979.

Moorhead, James. "Redefining Confessionalism: American Presbyterians in the Twentieth Century." In *The Confessional Mosaic: Presbyterians and Twentieth-Century Theology*, ed. M. Coalter, J. Mulder, and L. Weeks, 59–83. Louisville, Ken.: Westminster/John Knox Press, 1990.

Mulkay, Michael. *The Word and the World*. Cambridge, Eng.: Cambridge University Press, 1985.

Mumby, Dennis. *Communication and Power in Organizations*. Norwood, N.J.: Ablex Press, 1988.

Nelsen, Hart, Neil Cheek, and Paul Au. "Gender Differences in Images of God." *Journal for the Scientific Study of Religion* 24:396–402 (1985).

Niebuhr, H. Richard. *Christ and Culture*. New York: Harper & Brothers, 1951.

―――. "Religious Realism and the Twentieth Century." In *Religious Realism*, ed. D. C. MacIntosh. New York: Macmillan, 1931.

Noll, Mark. "God in the Colonies." In *Eerdmans' Handbook to Christianity in America*, ed. M. Noll, N. Hatch, G. Marsden, D. Wells, and J. Woodbridge, 1–154. Grand Rapids, Mich.: Eerdmans, 1983.

Numbers, Ronald. *The Creationists: The Evolution of Scientific Creationism*. New York: Knopf, 1992.

Peale, Norman Vincent. *The Power of Positive Thinking*. New York: Prentice-Hall, 1953.

Peshkin, Alan. *God's Choice: The Total World of a Fundamentalist Christian School*. Chicago: University of Chicago Press, 1986.

Piazza, Thomas, and Charles Glock. "Images of God and Their Social Meanings." In *The Religious Dimension: New Directions in Quantitative Research*, ed. R. Wuthnow, 69–91. New York: Academic Press, 1979.

Pilch, John. "Your Abba Is Not Your Daddy." *Modern Liturgy* 16:26 (1989).

Presbyterian Panel. *1991–1993 Background Report*. Louisville, Ken.: Presbyterian Church (U.S.A). Research Services, 1991.

Rogers, Carl. "A Theory of Therapy, Personality, and Interpersonal Relationships, as Developed in Client-Centered Frameworks." In *The Carl Rogers Reader*, ed. H. Kirschenbaum and V. Henderson, 236–62. Boston: Houghton Mifflin, 1959.

———. *On Becoming a Person*. Boston: Houghton Mifflin, 1961.

Rogers, Jack, and Donald McKim. "Pluralism and Policy in Presbyterian Views of Scripture." In *The Confessional Mosaic: Presbyterians and Twentieth-Century Theology*, ed. M. Coalter, J. Mulder, and L. Weeks, 37–58. Louisville, Ken.: Westminster/John Knox Press, 1990.

Roof, Wade C., and William McKinney. *American Mainline Religion*. New Brunswick, N.J.: Rutgers University Press, 1987.

Roof, Wade C., and Jennifer L. Roof. "Review of the Polls: Images of God among Americans." *Journal for the Scientific Study of Religion* 23:201–205 (1984).

Rosenberg, Bruce. *The Art of the American Folk Preacher*. New York: Oxford University Press, 1970.

Rosenberg, Ellen. *The Southern Baptists*. Knoxville: University of Tennessee Press, 1989.

Schuller, Robert. *Believe in the God Who Believes in You*. Nashville, Tenn.: Thomas Nelson, 1989.

———. *Self-Love*. Old Tappan, N.J.: Fleming H. Revell Company, 1969.

Simons, Herbert. "The Rhetoric of Inquiry as an Intellectual Movement." In *The Rhetorical Turn*, ed. H. Simons, 1–31. Chicago: University of Chicago Press, 1990.

Smith, Christine. *Weaving the Sermon: Preaching in a Feminist Perspective*. Louisville, Ken.: Westminster/John Knox Press, 1989.

Steimle, Edmund, Morris Niedenthal, and Charles Rice. *Preaching the Story*. Philadelphia: Fortress Press, 1980.

Steinfels, Peter. "Southern Baptists: Facing a Deep Rift." *New York Times* (May 14, 1991).

173

Steinfels, Peter. "Presbyterians Reject Report on Sex." *New York Times* (June 11, 1991).

Stout, Harry. *The New England Soul: Preaching and Religious Culture in Colonial New England*. New York: Oxford University Press, 1986.

Southern Baptist Convention, *1990 Southern Baptist Constituency Study*. Nashville, Tenn.: Sunday School Board of the Southern Baptist Convention, 1991.

Swidler, Ann. "Culture in Social Action: Symbols and Strategies." *American Sociological Review* 51:273–86 (1986).

Taylor, Charles. *Sources of the Self*. Cambridge, Mass.: Harvard University Press, 1989.

Tennant, F. R. *The Sources of the Doctrine of the Fall and Original Sin*. New York: Schocken, 1968.

Thompson, James, Jr. *Tried as by Fire: Southern Baptists and the Religious Controversies of the 1920s*. Macon, Ga.: Mercer University Press, 1982.

Tillich, Paul. *The Courage to Be*. New Haven, Conn.: Yale University Press, 1952.

———. *The Religious Situation*. New York: Meridian Books, 1932.

Tipton, Steven. *Getting Saved from the Sixties*. Berkeley: University of California Press, 1982.

Titon, Jeff. *Powerhouse for God*. Austin: University of Texas Press, 1988.

Tompkins, Philip, and George Cheney. "Communication and Unobtrusive Control in Contemporary Organizations." In *Organizational Communication: Traditional Themes and New Directions*, ed. R. McPhee and P. Tompkins, 179–210. Beverly Hills, Calif.: Sage, 1985.

Trinterud, Leonard. *The Forming of an American Tradition: A Reexamination of Colonial Presbyterianism*. Philadelphia: Westminster Press, 1949.

Tschannen, Olivier. "The Secularization Paradigm: A Systematization." *Journal for the Scientific Study of Religion* 30:395–415 (1991).

Van Zandt, David. *Living in the Children of God*. Princeton, N.J.: Princeton University Press, 1991.

Varenne, Henri. *Symbolizing America*. Lincoln: University of Nebraska Press, 1986.

Vergote, A., A. Tamayo, L. Pasquali, M. Bonami, M. Patyn, and A. Custers. "Concept of God and Parental Images." *Journal for the Scientific Study of Religion* 8:79–87 (1969).

Wallace, Walter. "Rationality, Human Nature, and Society in Weber's Theory." *Theory and Society* 19:199–223 (1990).

Warner, R. Steven. *New Wine in Old Wineskins: Evangelicals and Liberals in a Small-Town Church*. Berkeley: University of California Press, 1988.

Weber, Max. *The Protestant Ethic and the Spirit of Capitalism*. New York: Scribner's, 1958.

———. "Science as a Vocation." In *From Max Weber: Essays in Sociology*, ed. H. Gerth and C. W. Mills, 129–58. New York: Oxford University Press, 1946.

Wilson, Bryan. *Contemporary Transformations of Religion*. Oxford, Eng.: Oxford University Press, 1976.

————. *Religion in Secular Society: A Sociological Comment*. London: C. A. Watts, 1966.

Wuthnow, Robert. "Religious Beliefs and Experiences: Basic Patterns." In *Views from the Pews: Christian Beliefs and Attitudes*, ed. R. Johnson, 10–32. Philadelphia: Fortress Press, 1979.

————. *The Restructuring of American Religion*. Princeton, N.J.: Princeton University Press, 1988.

————. "Religious Discourse as Public Rhetoric." *Communication Research* 15:318–38 (1988).

————. *The Struggle for America's Soul: Evangelicals, Liberals, and Secularism*. Grand Rapids, Mich.: Eerdmans, 1989.

❖ Index ❖

Self: as arena of psychological "work," 20, 131–32; as child of God, 37–38, 117–18; essential qualities of, 107–19, 136; free will of, 108–9; innate goodness of, 110–11; and lack of fit in the world, 68–69; openness of, 111–14; Presbyterian views of, 136, 164n.15; and receptivity to God, 119–22; in relationship with others, 122–25; and self-disclosure, 112–14; Southern Baptist views of, 84–85, 106–28, 136, 162n.12; standardization of, 134–35; transformation of, 103–28; and trust, 112–14; as victim, 69, 74–75

Self-awareness, 114–18

Sermons. *See* Preaching

Sheilaism, 21

Sin, 50, 72, 79–102, 131, 136–39, 162n.13; as accretion on the self, 115–16; in children, 90–91, 102; civility in speech about, 82, 88–90, 95–97, 101–2, 160n.16; concrete identification of, 91; deflection of, 89–95, 101–2; depersonalization of, 89, 96; doctrines of, 33, 79–81, 104–5; euphemisms for, 162n.10; in Jews, 92–95, 102, 162n.15; mitigation of, 95–97; of the older brother, 85–87; of the prodigal son, 82–85; in propositional claims, 87; selective causality of, 89; in social underclass, 91–92; softening of talk about, 15, 20, 22; therapeutic tolerance of, 97–100; universality of, 87–89, 110

Sinners in the Hands of an Angry God, 79

Southern Baptist Convention: demographics of, 8, 147, 153n.15, 155n.33; expansion of, 8, 146–47; fundamentalists in, 8, 25, 146–48; history of, 144–48; moderates in, 8, 148

Swidler, Ann, 10. See also *Habits of the Heart*

Symbols, religious, 6, 16, 28–30, 138–40

Tertullian, 46, 164n.14

Tipton, Steven, 9. See also *Habits of the Heart*

Tolerance, 23, 97–100, 102

Trinity, 24, 36, 135, 159n.12

Warner, R. Steven, 9

Weber, Max, 6, 20

Wiesenthal, Simon, 94–95

World, 55–78, 116, 131; danger in, 70–75; enjoyment of, 59–64; human victimization in, 69, 74–75; lostness in, 57, 70–74; middle-class attitude toward, 65, 77; as pigpen, 57, 76–77, 123; pluralism of, 55–56, 67; as realm of meaninglessness, 57, 65–70; as source of separation from God, 57, 70–75; symbolic boundaries in, 65–66, 76, 78; as unproblematic for Christian faith, 57–65; as vehicle for self-awareness, 64

Wuthnow, Robert, 10, 18, 139, 158n.33